Air Battles Over Hungary 1944-45

Dmitriy Khazanov

Helion & Company

Helion & Company Limited
Unit 8 Amherst Business Centre
Budbrooke Road
Warwick
CV34 5WE
England
Tel. 01926 499 619
Email: info@helion.co.uk
Website: www.helion.co.uk
Twitter: @helionbooks
Visit our blog at blog.helion.co.uk

Published by Helion & Company 2021
Designed and typeset by Farr out Publications, Wokingham, Berkshire
Cover designed by Paul Hewitt, Battlefield Design (www.battlefield-design.co.uk)

ISBN 978-1-913336-20-2

British Library Cataloguing-in-Publication Data.
A catalogue record for this book is available from the British Library.

Contents

Acknowledgements

The author would like to extend his sincere thanks for the assistance in preparation of this book to the following individuals in Russian alphabetical order: Irina Bashnina, Dénes Bernád, Mikhail Bykov, Carl-Fredrik Geust, Vasiliy Golotyuk, Aleksander Medved, Yuriy Minkevich, Matti Salonen, Gennady Serov, Andrey Simonov, Aleksander Stykalin, Galina Tretyakova, Krisztian Ungvary, and all personnel of the reading hall of the Central Archive of the Russian Defence Ministry.

Photographs are provided courtesy of Russian State Documentary Film and Photo Archive, Central House of Aviation and Cosmonautics, Central Archive of the Russian Defence Ministry, and personal collections of Dénes Bernád, Csaba B. Stenge, Gennady Petrov, Mikhail Maslov, as well the author's private archive.

Introduction

The history of Hungary's joining of the war against the Soviet Union is rather peculiar. Before summer 1941, the two countries did not have any major controversies, territorial disputes or other problems that might mar their relations. However, Horthy's Hungary was, in terms of politics, well-disposed towards Hitler's Germany; the *Führer*, who actually set little store by Hungary's military potential, was quite content to have the country as the Reich's agricultural appendix and oil supplier. Hungary declared war on the USSR on 26 June 1941 after the strafing of a Hungarian train and an air bombardment of Košice. Allegedly, one of the dud bombs bore a marking showing that it had been manufactured by the Putilov plant in Leningrad (notwithstanding the fact that the plant in question had by that time been renamed!). We now know, however, that the provocative air raid was made by Romanian PZL-37 Łoś ('Elk') bombers.

It appears as if many high-ranking military officials had been waiting for this event: on the following day, the Hungarians delivered a 'vengeance strike' on the Soviet city of Stanislav (now Ivano-Frankovsk). Soon afterwards, a 25,000-strong 'mobile corps' with 'tankettes', armored vehicles and cannons, supported by outdated aircraft, engaged in battles on the southern flank of the Soviet–German front. In late November 1941, the remnants of the corps returned home, with matériel losses of nearly 100 percent and casualties (killed, missing or wounded) of nearly 50 percent of the initial military strength.

However, when Hitler was planning 1942's summer offensive, he demanded that Hungary, as an ally, provide two-thirds of its total armed forces for the operation. The Hungarians fought on non-critical sections of the southern flank of the Soviet–German front, where the rather well-trained but poorly armed and motivated Hungarian Second Army of 200,000 men won no laurels. The air force remained rather passive too, with its nearly 60 aircraft consolidated into the 1st Air Group, which was later (after replenishment with German aircraft) reformed into the 2nd Air Brigade. The Hungarian flyers were mostly engaged in reconnaissance operations, and suffered from the unreliable performance of their worn-out, obsolete aircraft and difficulties with repairs.

Initially, Hungary received rather positive news from the East. A series of raids made on military facilities in Budapest by long-range aircraft in late summer and early autumn 1942 hardly caused a serious blow to the spirit of the population, with the war still considered as being waged somewhere far away. However, matters then changed drastically. The encirclement of the German Sixth Army at Stalingrad was followed by several severe defeats for the *Wehrmacht* and its allies; the Hungarian Second Army, notable for the barbarous treatment of civilians by its soldiers, was defeated in the upper Don in January and early February 1943, suffering huge losses.

The Ukrainian historian A.V. Kotlobovsky summarized the results of the campaign as follows:

> The winter battles drew a line under the Don expedition of the *Honveds* [how the Hungarian soldiers were often referred to]. The results were far from joyful ones. The Air Force losses in January and February 1943 totaled at least 41 aircraft, most of which had to be destroyed by means of explosion in the course of a hurried retreat – this number was greater than losses for the entire second half-year in 1942. In total, in the course of the campaign in summer 1942 thru winter 1943, the Hungarian Air Force lost at least 62 aircraft. The casualties totaled 36 persons killed, 46 persons missing, 7 persons ill, 36 persons wounded, and 32 persons frostbitten. The remnants of units and detachments of the 2nd Air Brigade were scattered over the Ukrainian territory (in Kiev, Borispol, Vinnitsa, Konotop, Kharkov, and Poltava). The people were suffering the moral pressure of being defeated. The future looked gloomy.

Hungarian regent Vice-Admiral Miklós Horthy was among the first leaders of Hitler's allies to realize the inevitability of defeat for the Axis powers. He began clandestine negotiations with the Allies of the anti-Hitler coalition, but these led to no actual results. At the time, the Hungarian Air Force, which was gradually being refitted with German aircraft, remained in Soviet territory, despite Hitler's order in spring 1943 to remove Hungarian forces from the front and have them acting only as guards in occupied territories. For about a year, the Hungarian aviation kept on conducting warfare more or less successfully on the Eastern Front; later, the soldiers returned to their home country.

During the period from summer 1942 to March 1944, the *Luftwaffe*'s *Luftflotte 4* (4th Air Fleet) transferred 164 aircraft to Hungarian units and detachments in the East, including 56 Bf 109Gs and 51 Ju 88A/C/Ds. Active preparations for repelling attacks by the Western Allies' air forces coincided with a cooling-down in German–Hungarian relations. In response to Horthy's attempts to find a way out of the war and sign an armistice in the West and the East, the German command decided to take anticipatory measures. Horthy's assurances at negotiations in Berlin to the effect that Hungary would never start military activities against Germany made no impression whatsoever on Hitler. Indeed, in the early hours of 19 March 1944, on the *Führer*'s command, 11 *Wehrmacht* divisions crossed the Hungarian border and soon completed the country's occupation. However, despite this, the majority of the population still treated the Germans as allies.

In spring 1944, the US and British air forces commenced saturation raids on Hungarian territory to eliminate military plants and railway networks, disrupt the operation of oil refineries and undermine the population's morale. Soon, the Hungarians had to draw a considerable number of their fighters (eventually all the fighters which were at their disposal) and anti-aircraft artillery to fight off these raids. On the morning on 3 April, 180 four-engine bombers of the 15th US Army Air Force – escorted by 170 fighters – delivered a massive attack on the Danube Aviation Plant in the vicinity of Budapest. The raid, which killed over 1,000 civilians, made a strong impression on both the population and Hungarian pilots, who had never until then faced such power.

From late summer to early autumn1944, long-range air force formations began operations against Hungarian facilities, but could use only limited resources. This was because the Soviet long-range aviation's principal targets were then located in the Baltic region (where such ports as Libau, Memel and Riga underwent systematic raids) and East Prussia. Long-range bombers made many sorties to support the uprising in Slovakia, supplying the insurgents with multifarious weapons and ammunition, and Marshal Josef Tito's partisans of the National Liberation Army of Yugoslavia, providing them with everything they needed to fight the occupying Axis forces. After an almost two-year break, the first Soviet saturation raid against targets in Hungary was made during the night of 13/14 September, when bombs were dropped on Budapest. The bombers targeted military and industrial facilities in the Hungarian capital, including the old fortress area, the military barracks, the machine-building plant, and the gas works. The bombardment resulted in 25 major fires across the capital.

According to German sources, a raid on the following night was even more successful. The Soviet *Informbureau* reported:

> On the night before 15 September, our long-range aircraft again performed a mass raid on the Hungarian capital Budapest. The bombardment of military industrial facilities in Budapest resulted in over 35 fires, among them up to 20 large ones. The observers noted bombs hitting a bridge across the Danube. Major explosions occurred in the west railway station in the territory of principal railway shops, in the machine-building plant, and at other facilities in the city. Our pilots could see the flame of the fires from a distance of 250km while leaving the target area.

The IL-4s of the Soviet III Army Corps appeared in the skies above Hungary more often than other aircraft. It was these aircraft that attacked aerodromes around the Hungarian capital such as those at Budaörs, Csepel, Ferihegy and Matyasfeld, damaging runways and around 10 vehicles, and causing the explosion of a refueling truck. On the night of 15/16 September, up to 50 fires were caused by raids in Debrecen, with the largest blaze at the railway station, where four troop trains were damaged or burnt. Three days later, another railway station, that at Tschop (Csap), 25km to the south of Uzhgorod, also came under attack, with severe damage to storage facilities used by the Germans and Hungarians.

Soviet aviators from the 26th and 27th Guards Regiments (known as 'Hunters/Blockers') acted vigorously and with success in this direction. For example, on the night of 16/17 September, the Deputy Commander of the 27th Regiment, Major N.A. Krapiva, who was one of the most experienced and well-trained pilots and an initiator of the application of the Automatic Combined Artillery Battery (ACAB) on A-20G aircraft, flew over the enemy's aerodromes near Budapest. While patrolling at a low altitude, he noticed a Bf 109 fighter, approached it, and shot it down by cannon fire from behind. In total that month, the Soviet long-range air forces made six raids on Budapest, Debrecen, Tschop and other major cities, primarily causing damage to railway stations and terminals of the last ally of Hitler's Germany.

The target geography in Hungary brought about an unpleasant episode in the biography of the Soviets' Long-Range Air Force Commander, Marshal A.E. Golovanov. He had relied on his own memory and failed to write down, in his notebook, the instructions of Stalin, the Supreme Commander-in-Chief. "Cities, regions and settlements in Hungary bear hardly pronounceable and, consequently, hard-to-remember – for us Russians – names," Golovanov remembered later. "Of the five targets that Stalin ordered to be subject to saturated raids on each consequent night, the fourth one escaped my memory." Studying a detailed map did not help him. Luckily for Golovanov, by the time it came to the fourth target, the need to make a raid on it had disappeared, and the Supreme Commander-in-Chief had ordered their bombs to be dropped at a different location.

After the anti-fascist *coup d'état* in Romania, Hungary had to face not only the Red Army, the Red Army Air Force and the powerful air forces of the Western Allies, but also a new enemy, Romania, which wished to take back (with the assistance of Soviet forces) the portion of Transylvania it had lost in autumn 1940 under the Second Vienna Award (also known as the Vienna *Diktat*, under which the Nazis arbitrated over territorial disputes in lands they controlled). In response, the Hungarians managed to strengthen their air force by hastily forming new units. The Hungarian leaders also enhanced their diplomatic maneuvering to bring the country out of the war with minimum losses; however, once again such efforts were unsuccessful. Meantime, the front line was inexorably approaching the territory of the last European ally of Hitler's Germany.

1

Debrecen Offensive

The close of summer 1944 was marked by the Red Army's triumph on the southern flank of the Soviet–German front. The brilliant Yassy-Kishinev Offensive ended with the encirclement of a major enemy formation; Romania (as mentioned above) left the war and ceased to be a member of the Axis powers, and soon declared war on Germany. Meanwhile, the Bulgarian populace greeted the Soviet army as if it were that of a brother state, and Bulgaria also joined the anti-Hitler coalition. Soviet troops, together with detachments of the National Liberation Army of Yugoslavia, also started expelling German forces from Yugoslavia. The major role in all these operations was played by the troops of the 2nd and 3rd Ukrainian Front, under the command of Marshals R.Y. Malinovsky and F.I. Tolbukhin, who then carried out military activities in Hungary.

The Soviet command planned to develop the offensive in several directions; first and foremost, it expected to defeat the enemy in the central portion of Hungary. The liberation of Hungary from Nazism started on 23 September 1944, with troops of the 2nd Ukrainian Front entering its territory. The *Wehrmacht* command understood that the loss of Hungary would open the route to Austria and southern Germany for the Red Army. Hungary also still remained a base for German industry: it had a major bauxite field and was one of the principal oil sources (after the loss of Romanian oil) and an agricultural products supplier. Therefore, Hitler was determined to keep Hungary among his allies at all costs.

Throughout September, the German command headed by Colonel General J. Friessner in the south of the Eastern Front made desperate attempts to 'stabilize' (in fact, to gather anew the remnants of defeated troops) a new, almost 1,000km-long, front. The German command, now designated Army Group South, had serious concerns about the Red Army's ability to march, together with the Romanians, through Hungary and Slovakia in just two or three weeks and to terminate the war by a strike on the Reich from the south. Besides, the Hungarian Army at the time was far from demonstrating a readiness to fight 'to the last soldier'. A major role in increasing the power of Army Group South was played by the *Luftwaffe*: throughout September 1944, the strength of *Luftflotte 4* under the command of Colonel General O. Dessloch grew by some 50 percent to total nearly 600 aircraft.

The Soviets had an air force up to three times that size. Deputy Commander of one of the divisions of the 5th Air Army, Lieutenant Colonel B.N. Yeremin, clarified the reasons why this advantage was not made full use of:

> In autumn, conditions in highlands tend to change often and quite abruptly. We had a limited network of aerodromes, and it was difficult to find a suitable airfield. Somehow at first I thought that after crossing the Carpathian Mountains we would find ourselves in a flat land. Nothing of the sort! The greater portion of Romania consists of highlands. The mountains are not high; however, troops have difficulties with advancing. There are almost no places for deployment; we had to walk and drive mostly in narrow tortuous valleys. In such circumstances, the air force's tasks become complicated. In each sortie, pilots have to face various difficulties including low clouds, dense strips of fog hiding the land, and limited opportunities for a forced landing. However, we might not cancel reconnaissance missions.

Luftwaffe documents contain many complaints in respect of bad weather conditions and problems with airbases. Heavy rains and waterlogged airfields brought considerable complications for combat air force operations. Both the Germans and Hungarians used the Messerschmitt Bf 109G as their principal fighter type. Despite all the good points of this aircraft, they had poor landing components and often met with various flight accidents, even when being piloted by leading fighter aces. For example, *Oberleutnant* H. Lipfert of the *II/JG52* Fighter Wing, who had just returned from leave and had, by that time, achieved 145 victories, barely survived one crash. Lipfert later recalled:

> I tried to taxi to take-off position, but the wheels were so deeply stuck in the soaked soil that the aircraft could not get out by itself. It was towed to the runway start; in the process, the radiators were splashed with mud to such an extent that the service personnel had to thoroughly clean them before take-off. I started the take-off run, but my Messer accelerated only slightly during the first 100m of the take-off run; there was almost no increase in speed. What was even worse – the aircraft was swinging considerably and could nose over at any moment. After a few manipulations

with the control stick, the 109 lifted off, but at the very same moment its left wheel suddenly lowered ... Soon the left wing was almost touching the ground, and I saw a Bf 110 dashing towards me from the opposite direction. The collision seemed inevitable, but suddenly my aircraft miraculously leveled off and touched the ground with all three wheels. But here I ran into another Messerschmitt. There were two huge hits, and then I found myself sitting under the open sky. Before my fighter stopped I noticed that it had lost the left wing, and the aft portion of the fuselage was not there anymore. The parked Hungarian Bf 100 also was considerably damaged.

To prevent Soviet forces from entering Hungary, the *Wehrmacht* command planned a series of counterstrikes. A directive of the German Army's General Staff of 30 September 1944 ordered Army Group South to hold the Carpathian ledge (against the 4th Ukrainian Front) and, at the same time, to prepare an offensive operation to deliver a strike from the Debrecen area against the Red Army troops which had reached the border between Oradea and Mako, and to "close on such an objective as might be reasonably held by a modest force during the winter [1944–45]". The Germans strove to use mobile divisions with *Luftwaffe* support to defeat the left wing of the 2nd Ukrainian Front and, after a redeployment, to deliver a strike on the right wing of the Front. If succeeding with this plan, the German command hoped to close the Soviet passage to northern Transylvania and the Middle Danube Valley. At the same time, German divisions were being withdrawn to Hungary from southern regions of Yugoslavia, Albania, and Greece.

Meantime, the principal forces of the 2nd Ukrainian Front left Yassy and Kishinev far behind, and, with support from the 5th Air Army (though documents report only a negligible number of mission sorties before 6 October), marched round the eastern edge of the Carpathians and entered the reaches of the Lower Danube Valley. The Soviet troops continued the offensive and, in early October 1944, their left wing entered Yugoslavia and crossed the Romanian–Hungarian boundary. The territory on the right (to the east of the Dukla Pass) right up to the Romanian border saw heavy fighting involving the 4th Ukrainian Front. Troops of the 3rd Ukrainian Front were fighting on the left in Yugoslavia.

Preparations for the 2nd Ukrainian Front troops' further offensive began in Romania in early September, with reinforcing units (the *Stavka*'s, i.e. the Soviet High Command's, standby forces) brought up from the rear. In particular, the 5th Air Army, which was essentially part of Marshal Malinovsky's front, was reinforced by the 5th Attack Air Regiment (of the 4th Guards Division and the 264th Attack Division, plus the 331st Fighter Division) under the command of one of the first Heroes of the Soviet Union, General N.P. Kamanin, and by the 6th Guards Fighter Division, commanded by Colonel I.I. Geibo, which had somewhat earlier been transferred from the 2nd Air Army. Meanwhile, in late September, the 10th Guards Attack Division was moved to the 17th Air Army of the 3rd Ukrainian Front, which was on the offensive nearby; later, together with the 236th Fighter Division, it formed the backbone of the Soviet air group in Yugoslavia. Support forces had to overcome huge difficulties to prepare logistic bases, whereas the headquarters worked on the issues of interaction between combined-arms units and air forces.

Without operational pause, the 2nd Ukrainian Front started the Debrecen Offensive Operation in an endeavor to break through to the Danube Valley in Hungary. The Germans managed to prepare for such a course of events by concentrating two fresh *panzer* divisions near the front and arranging a counterattack. This resulted in an encounter tank battle during which both sides' air forces were active, especially those of the Soviets, with fighters patrolling the battlefield in several tiers, while ground-attack aircraft, in groups of six to eight, delivered strikes on the enemy in several crucial areas. Occasionally, Soviet pilots also strafed the enemy's aerodromes.

The assumption that hostilities had opened between Hungary and Romania was confirmed. However, in September the Romanians suffered extremely heavy losses in battles with the *Luftwaffe*, with the greatest damage suffered by the 2nd and 6th Fighter Groups, which had been flying IAR81 aircraft. At the outset of the Debrecen Operation, activity by the Romanian air corps was only slight; this was attributed to bad weather and the need to enhance the units' battle-worthiness. The Romanian crews mostly took part in strafing attacks and bombings of enemy troops, during which they suffered from fire by Soviet anti-aircraft gunners, who knew the silhouettes of the Bf 109, Ju 87, Ju 88 and Hs 129 aircraft they were operating perfectly well and commenced effective fire whenever such aircraft appeared in the sky.

Senior Lieutenant K.S. Maltsev, a young Soviet pilot of the 177th Guards Fighter Regiment, covered himself with glory in these battles. Documents record that he joined the front-line forces in May that year and was awarded the first Order of the Red Banner in early October after 34 combat sorties for his skilled and high-quality photographing of the enemy's troops and matériel during the course of reconnaissance operations. While escorting troops on 6 October, Maltsev brought down in air combat two FW 190s and a Bf 109. During the course of a covering operation on the following day, his group met 40 Ju 87s and up to 10 FW 190S. According to the after-action report:

> The group of six La-5s had, beyond the covering mission, also the task to bomb the enemy. As soon as the bombs (which were set to 'unarmed') were dropped, our group engaged in air combat. Due to defective bomb-release gear, Comrade Maltsev's bombs remained under the wing; in this configuration, he was fighting the battle, and brought down a FW 190 and a Ju 87.

Major S.A. Matvienko's 179th Guards Fighter Regiment also fought efficiently. Singular dedication among the regiment's pilots was demonstrated by one of the most efficient fighter aces of the entire III Guards Fighter Corps, A.A. Dyakov, who had shortly before the Debrecen events been reduced to the ranks for a criminal offense. A Ju 87, which was brought down by him on 6 October, became the pilot's 27th victory. According to land forces commanders, the key role in the land battles for Debrecen was played by the 7th Guards Attack Division under the command of Lieutenant Colonel G.P. Shuteyev. All three regiments of the division (Guards Regiments 130, 131 and 132) were replenished with the newest Il-10s, which exceeded their predecessor Il-2s in speed by approximately 100km/h at all altitudes and had better maneuverability and more powerful attack and defensive weapons.

The battles at this time were uncompromising. The German–Hungarian formations repeatedly took counteroffensive measures, with support from their air forces, and both sides suffered heavy losses. "On 10 October, we managed to cut off three of the enemy's tank and mechanized corps, which had broken through to the north, from their support," wrote Colonel General Friessner. "Warfare against this Soviet formation and against the forces attacking our switching defensive line grew into a knockdown tank battle under Debrecen, with its outcome to exert the decisive influence on the entire situation in Hungary."

Meanwhile, the concentration of German *panzer* forces was completed in the region east of Szolnok and west of Debrecen. These armoured units were tasked with defeating Russian tank and mechanized troops by means of converging counterattacks and thus preventing the development of the breakthrough. Both sides reported that the ensuing tank battle was extremely violent, with its intensity as high as that of the Battle of Kursk in June the previous year. Consequently, the two German *panzer* divisions affected a linkup near the town of Püspökladány on the road between Szolnok and Debrecen, thus cutting off the mobile troops of the 2nd Ukrainian Front from their principal forces. However, the German command failed to develop the initial success, so Friessner's prediction of the battle having a "decisive influence on the entire situation in Hungary" proved false.

During the course of the mobile fighting, the Red Army, whilst holding back the enemy, kept on delivering strikes on various segments of the German defenses, which turned out to be poorly prepared for such a course of action. The amount of matériel captured by Soviet troops was huge; it should be noted that the number of aircraft captured on the ground was considerably higher than those brought down in air battles or through actions of anti-aircraft gunners. Thus, for example, near Nádudvar, General Pliyev's cavalry captured 80 enemy aircraft, all of them unable to fly due to being without wheels. A Hungarian aerodrome with 60 aircraft was also captured near Szolnok. According to another report, a vanguard unit of the 297th Rifle Division (of the 7th Guards Army), which was carrying out operations near Kecskemét, "dispersed the garrison of the city, burnt 35 aircraft at the aerodrome, blew up 2 fuel depots and 2 ammunition depots, destroyed the post office and telegraph building, and then returned to Csongrád".

Situation reports of the Red Army's General Headquarters reveal that the number of German aircraft flyovers at the time of the intense encounter battle was considerably higher than the number of sorties made by the 5th Air Army, except on 13 and 14 October, when the ratio was 423 to 140 in the Soviets' favor. On the following day (15 October), the Soviet pilots made 250 sorties, while their enemy's air forces responded with 500 flyovers (according to German data, over 700 sorties were made, with the Ju 87s, Hs 129s, and FW 190s particularly active) in groups of up to 50 aircraft. Often without any cover, these groups strafed the fighting formations of the 6th Guards Tank Army and the groups of Generals I.A. Pliyev and S.I. Gorshkov. However, on 16 October, the troops of the 2nd Ukrainian Front successfully captured the city of Oradea-Mare and encircled and then defeated a Hungarian combat group between the Sebes-Köros and Berettyó canals. According to reports, the enemy's losses were huge. Over 9,650 troops were taken as POWs; the captured matériel included 29 tanks and assault guns, 222 pieces of field artillery ordnance, 91 aircraft, 20 troop trains (partially with platforms) and 17 steam locomotives.

The intelligence section of the 5th Air Army Headquarters then received important information regarding the enemy. Before being delegated to Bucharest to act as a member of the Soviet Control Commission, Deputy Chief of Section Lieutenant Colonel V.M. Kuryshev summarized the results of examinations of POWs and line-crossers for the first half of October 1944. At the time, the Hungarians provided much interesting information. As a rule, pilots together with staff officers flew over to the Soviet side on Fi 156, FW 58 or Go 145 aircraft, and willingly gave evidence and provided available maps or other documents. A Do 217M long-range reconnaissance aircraft of the *1(F)/Nacht* unit also flew over to the Soviet side on 8 October, but for a different reason: the crew of the aircraft lacked experience, lost their bearings at night, landed at a Soviet aerodrome, and gave themselves up as prisoners to Flight Control Officer Major Biryukov, who had approached the aircraft.

Another POW who provided valuable information was *Feldwebel* H. Rosenberg of the *III/JG77* (documents reveal that the pilot had shortly before been transferred *Gruppe* to *II/JG52*). He was an experienced pilot who had made 140 combat sorties and brought down three American aircraft. His *Gruppe*, which was equipped with battered Messerschmitt Bf 109G-6s, had been preparing to leave the Vienna Seyring aerodrome for Germany in order to be replenished and re-equipped with the advanced Bf 109G-14 and K-4 fighters. The *III/JG77* was under the command of Captain A. Köhler, and its top fighter ace was Lieutenant H. Hackler, who was credited with 56 victories (37 according to German documents). "We made our last sorties from the Liec airfield near the Tisza riverbed," Rosenberg said. "Because the front line advanced quickly in this area, the group had to change the base often. Thus, we stayed only for a day at the Bervel aerodrome, and for just as long at Debrecen. All this affected our battleworthiness; by 15 October, the group had been reduced to two units, with 22 Messerschmitts left."

The Soviet command was striving to intensify air operations. Observing the actions of his subordinates on 18 October, the commander of the II Attack Corps, Lieutenant General V.V. Stepichev, observed:

> The battle [for Debrecen, where the enemy brought into action an SS tank division and an SS motorized division, both fresh formations] was often decided in a few seconds; the battle was not infrequently turned into a duel between the cavalry of General I.A. Pliyev [Cavalry Mechanized Group Pliyev was in the vanguard of the offensiv] and the Tigers and Panthers attacking them head-on. That is where our ground-attack aircraft did their 'holy business': a precision series of anti-tank air bombs and short-distance cannon shots by such pilots as I.V. Nikitin and I.V. Klevtsov and others opened the way for the advance of the Cossacks.

On 20 October, Soviet tank troops, together with the cavalry and with support from ground-attack aircraft and fighters of the 5th Air Army, broke into Debrecen. Over 1,000 soldiers and officers were taken as POWs; the day was also rich in captured matériel, among which was 49 defective aircraft, 12 operable aircraft, 13 steam locomotives, 10 storage depots and 23 railway troop trains, some of which included platforms with aircraft and tanks on them. It should be added that the Debrecen aerodrome was, in early autumn 1944, stuffed with miscellaneous matériel, it being the place where the Germans had evacuated aircraft from Romania after the *coup d'état* there. Shortly before the arrival of the Soviet troops, ground-attack aircraft of the US 15th Air Army had delivered several devastating strikes on the Debrecen aerodrome, with the most severe damage inflicted on the *I/KG4* unit. There were so many abandoned aircraft because the Germans had no time to remove them for repair or recycling. In the evening, Supreme Commander-in-Chief Joseph Stalin ordered a 20-salvo salute be given to the troops of the 2nd Ukrainian Front and made specific mention of the airmen of the 7th Guards Attack Division and 177th Guards Fighter Regiment by conferring on them the honorable title of 'Debrecen Division' and 'Debrecen Regiment', respectively.

The II Attack Corps of Lieutenant General Stepichev achieved particular success in these military operation and was the last unit during the war on which the right to style itself a 'Guards Corps' was conferred by Order of the People's Commissar for Defense No.340 of 27 October 1944. Before spring 1944, the II Attack Corps carried out operations in eastern Byelorussia around Vitebsk and Orsha. From April 1944, it was withdrawn from the 1st Air Army and transferred to the 2nd Ukrainian Front, where, before the Uman-Botoşani offensive, it was included in the 5th Air Army. At the time the corps consisted of two divisions: the 7th Guards Attack Division (commanded by Lieutenant Colonel G.P. Shuteyev) and the 231st Attack Division (Colonel L.A. Chizhikov); the latter, under the abovementioned Order, was transformed into the 12th Guards Attack Division. The 568th, 873rd and 570th Attack Regiments were from then on referred to as the 187th, 188th and 190th Guards Attack Regiments, respectively. A few days later, the corps received the 279th Fighter Division, which was led by Colonel V.G. Blagoveshchensky. This division had earlier been used to provide cover for ground-attack aircraft. Its inclusion in the II Air Corps was aimed at improving cooperation and reducing losses.

Looking further ahead, throughout October 1944 the crews of General S.K. Goryunov's 5th Air Army made 8,400 mission sorties; of these, 953 were for air reconnaissance purposes. Air reconnaissance was carried out, along with special-purpose reconnaissance units (such as the 511th Separate Reconnaissance Regiment and 207th Separate Spotter and Reconnaissance Regiment), by crews of the III Guards Attack Corps and 6th Guards Fighter Division. Land-based command headquarters and the 5th Air Army headquarters thereby received, on a regular basis, information on the advance of Soviet troops, defense fortifications, the enemy's maneuvers, and formations of their tank troops, all of which was extremely important. Of the total number of mission sorties, 2,200 were made by pilots of the 5th Air Army from 13–20 October, during the most intense period of the battle for Debrecen.

By now the Axis forces, to avoid defeat and to withdraw their troops, had to prepare a counterstrike using tanks and motorized formations. Neither were the German air forces passive at this time. According to the Red Army Air Force Intelligence Department, the *Luftwaffe*'s activity along the Soviet–German front decreased by approximately 30 percent between September and October, and mostly consisted of delivering air strikes on land troops, counteracting operations by Soviet air forces and conducting reconnaissance. The highest activity was observed by the 1st Baltic Front, 2nd Belorussian Front and 2nd Ukrainian Front (in Hungary). Out of the total of 11,831 mission sorties made by the Germans and Hungarians, 14 percent (1,679 sorties) were made against formations in Marshal Malinovsky's 2nd Ukrainian Front. However, on certain days the front-line Air Observation, Warning and Communication stations registered up to 500 flyovers by German and Hungarian aircraft above narrow sections of the front, more than the number of mission sorties performed by the Soviet Air Force.

Approximately 10 percent of all *Luftwaffe* sorties were performed at night. Here, the principal amount of work was done by the *NSGr5* under the command of Major J. Boellner. One of the tasks to be performed by the Axis air forces at night or in bad weather conditions consisted of mine-laying along the Danube. Usually, Heinkel aircraft of the *KG4* wing were used as mine carriers. Thus, for example, during the night of 16/17 October, between 18 and 20 BM1000 non-contact mines were dropped in the waters of the Danube near Corabia and Zimnicea. As a result, boat traffic in this area was temporarily stopped, and ships and boats of the Soviets' Danube Military Flotilla had to carry out minesweeping duties. It should be noted that many mines were also dropped in the Danube in the summer and autumn of 1944 by English and American aircraft, and all those mines had to be neutralized too.

Only the 2nd Ukrainian Front witnessed strikes on Soviet aerodromes, which were made by units of six to nine Ju 87s and six to 12 FW 190s, under the cover of pairs of Bf 109s. First, the Junkers delivered a strike by dropping high-explosive bombs and a large number of fragmentation bombs, which were referred to by the Soviets as 'frogs'. Then, the Focke-Wulfs attacked aircraft parking areas using gun and cannon fire. Several 'converging axis' attacks on aerodromes were made by He 111s, which approached an airfield from two or three directions and delivered strikes on aircraft and aerodrome buildings in partially cloudy conditions. The Germans also repeatedly used units of between six and 12 fighters to block the operation of Soviet fighters (generally during bombing and strike attack on land troops), approaching the Yakovlev and Lavochkin aircraft in advance and preventing them from taking off upon receiving orders from the command post.

According to *Luftwaffe* sources, throughout October its 4th Air Fleet destroyed 112 Soviet aircraft; of these, 64 aircraft were brought down in aerial battles by Bf 109 fighters or FW 190 ground-attack aircraft, 10 were shot down by *Luftwaffe* anti-aircraft gunners and 38 were destroyed or burnt on the ground. (The Soviets acknowledged the loss of only eight aircraft on the ground, including three Polikarpov Po-2s; according to the Germans, the Red Army's bombing and strike attacks resulted in the loss of just one parked German aircraft along the entire Soviet–German front). One of the leading German fighter aces, *Oberleutnant* H. Lipfert, recalled a raid during the early morning of 28 October on an aerodrome near Debrecen, where Soviet fighters and ground-attack aircraft had been redeployed shortly before:

> The beginning of the day was gloomy and rainy; however, later ideal weather established [itself] for a sudden ground attack. Soon we took off and headed south-east in a combat formation. Along a wide arc, we flew southward, and approached the aerodrome from the east keeping just under the ceiling edge of continuous clouds, which in the morning of that day were at an altitude of 2,500m. As soon as Debrecen emerged from the fog at a distance, group commander *Major* G. Barkhorn ordered, 'Close up, keep close formation, attack!'
>
> A Russian communication aircraft flew near the aerodrome right before us. However, our attention was not sidetracked by it; instead, we kept flying toward our target at a high speed. One can only imagine the bewilderment of Russian pilots; they had no chance to get into their fighters and start the engines, because we appeared before they became aware of danger. In descent, I leveled off my plane until I was 50m above the ground and caught the target (a Yakovlev aircraft) in the gunsight. I fired from a distance of about 100m and saw hitting flashes sparkling all over the fuselage of the enemy's aircraft. Only a short glance was enough to state that the Yak was burning.
>
> Then I turned to the other side of the aerodrome where the hangars were. I saw tracer streaks stretching in my direction; nevertheless, I managed to strike another parked fighter and a hangar. A moment later the airfield was behind me. To avoid anti-aircraft fire, I kept at a low altitude. Meanwhile, my group within a minute climbed and turned around. We returned to the aerodrome. This time, the anti-aircraft artillery gave us a 'warm reception'. But we again descended and continued our mission. Luckily for us, none of the Russian fighters took off, because we had too little fuel to engage in air combat. From a considerable distance, I viewed the burning aircraft, and counted approximately 12 of them [in fact, the losses totaled three communication aircraft]. Some of our fighters were hit, but miraculously none of them was lost.

The Soviet command decided to precede the new stage of the offensive with a raid by front-line aircraft on Budapest. On the order of the Deputy Commander of the 5th Air Army, General V.I. Smirnov, two attack groups (one Soviet and oneRomanian), with 25 aircraft in each, were prepared for the sortie. It should be noted that the Romanians, now allies of the USSR in the anti-Hitler coalition, were fighting as part of the 2nd Ukrainian Front. "Marshal Malinovsky only trusted the Romanian army to a very small extent," the Hungarian historian P. Gostoni observed: "As soon as the Romanians reached their national goal by taking Transylvania back, their martial ardor waned considerably."

Indeed, the war-weary Romanians were not in the least attracted by the campaign in Hungary. Furthermore, their holding power, even against minor local attacks of the Germans, left much to be desired. On the other hand, their relations with the Hungarians became much worse after several combats on the ground and in the air in early autumn 1944. Thereafter, the USSR's new allies decided to take part in the planned sortie, and the commander of the Romanian I Air Corps, E. Ionescu, was ordered to provide 25 Ju 88s of the 5th Bomber Group. The Soviets assigned 25 of their best-trained Boston crews (the Red Army Air Force received around 3,000 Douglas A-20 'Boston' medium bombers from the US through the Lend-Lease scheme) from the 218th Bomber Division; the unit's commander, Colonel N.K. Romanov, was expected to lead the crews himself during the sortie and was appointed commander of the entire group. Training was conducted under an extremely tight schedule, but by the morning of the raidf, all 50 crews were ready and waiting for the signal to start. A witness from the 5th Air Army headquarters recalled:

> There was only one thing left to be done, that is, to order that the bomber group should start out for the combat sortie, but everything went wrong because of a dense fog which was blanketing the southern portion of Transylvania and, according to Air Reconnaissance, the [entirety of] Budapest as well. We were waiting impatiently for the fog to melt away and kept constantly in touch with the airborne reconnaissance aircraft, but always received only one answer, 'It is still foggy.' Finally, General Zakharov had nothing else to do but report to Moscow, 'The departure is impossible ... ' Thus we had to transfer the bomber group to Nyíregyháza, which was a large railway and highway hub.

The Budapest offensive was expected to begin immediately after the Debrecen offensive, without any operational rest. Consequently, preparations in the headquarters of the 5th Air Army were carried out in hectic conditions. Given that the final updates were made to the plan at the very last moment, the aviation specialists did not have a wink of sleep while working with maps. The situation was further aggravated by the commander's illness: V.A. Sudets resumed his duties only the night before the new offensive. The chief of the Control Headquarters of the 5th Air Army, General S.N. Grechko, recalled: "Preparation for the new offensive was being developed simultaneously [by all elements of the air army]; it was a continuous process without a moment's rest ... [Chief of Staff] General N.G Seleznev showed himself a brilliant leader. Before dark, we, with his direct participation, completed the preparation of the air offensive and the combat sortie schedule for the groups."

At the time, Hungary was witnessing important political events. The Germans had learned the lessons taught them by the governments of Bulgaria and especially Romania, their former comrades-in-arms who in autumn 1944 had turned their weapons on Germany. The Germans were now carefully watching the political maneuvers of the Hungarian administration. Regent Miklós Horthy made no secret of his peaceful aspirations, and on 15 October he addressed the Hungarian people with a statement to the effect that the country should immediately withdraw from the war. However, the Regent's move lacked comprehensive preparation. Within 24 hours, a large group of German troops including over 600 tanks entered Budapest. The Germans established control over the city's basic infrastructure facilities, and quickly quelled the resistance of the Regent's supporters. Horthy was forced to recognize the authority of the leader of the right-wing radical Arrow Cross Party, Ferenc Szálasi, who had been selected by the Germans. The issue of continuing the war was thus no longer on the Hungarian agenda.

The Soviet command recognised that the Axis forces had created heavily protected defensive lines along the approaches to Budapest; however, it believed that they had evidently not enough forces to protect the capital. Moscow gave Marshal Malinovsky the task of defeating their enemy's troops and taking Hungary out of the war. The left wing of the 2nd Ukrainian Front was to promptly initiate the offensive in the area between the Tisza and Danube rivers in order to forestall the Axis reinforcement of Budapest and inflict decisive losses. The ground forces were to be supported by the 5th Air Army of General Goryunov, whose actions were of critical importance to the operation. According to Soviet documents, the number of opposing aerial forces as of 20 October 1944 was as follows:

5th Air Army			Total German–Hungarian Air Force
	Total	In good condition	
Fighters	430	371	160
Ground-attack aircraft	132	130	220
Bombers	185	180	120
Reconnaissance and spotter aircraft	37	34	50
Total	**784**	**715**	**550**

The above correlation, however, does not include the aircraft of the Soviet 17th Air Army, which were expected to be employed in the offensive after helping in the liberation of Yugoslavia. On 20 October 1944, troops of the 3rd Ukrainian Front and the National Liberation Army of Yugoslavia, supported by the ships of the Danube Military Flotilla, had captured the ancient fortress of Kalemegdan, the last German stronghold in Belgrade, and thus liberated the Yugoslav capital. The successful completion of the Belgrade offensive resulted in the defeat of Gerrmany's Army Group Serbia and liberation of Serbian territory. The table below illustrates the total number of aircraft the 17th Air Army had available for operations in Hungary at the end of October and their breakdown per type:

17th Air Army			
	Type	Total	In good condition
Fighters	La-5	250	238
	Yak-9, Yak-3	272	260
Ground-attack aircraft	Il-2	472	440
Bombers	A-20B, B-III	115	107
Night bombers	Polikarpov Po-2	119	115
Reconnaissance aircraft	Petlyakov Pe-2	23	21
	Yaovlev Yak-9	11	11
Spotters	Il-2	20	20
	Yak-9	12	12
Total		**1,294**	**1,224**

Throughout Hungary, the Soviet Air Force had an approximately threefold numerical superiority over their opponents, taking into account the aircraft of the Hungarian Air Force. In terms of combat-ready aircraft, the numerical superiority was at least fourfold. In an attempt to coordinate actions and to use air groups with maximum efficiency, the *Luftwaffe* created the so-called 'Fighter Command in Hungary', which included German day and night fighter units and (later) Hungarian fighters and fighter-bombers. Renowned German fighter ace Major G. Schoepfel became head of the Fighter Command. According to German sources, the *Luftwaffe*'s 4th Air Fleet had the following aircraft at its disposal as of 2 November 1944:

4th Air Fleet		
	Total	In good condition
Single-engine fighters	89	63
Night fighters	59	22
Day ground-attack aircraft	187	130
Night ground-attack aircraft	45	26
Bombers	63	40
Long-range and short-range reconnaissance aircraft	53	20
Total	**496**	**301**

Note: Except bombers, night fighters and long-range reconnaissance aircraft, all other units were part of the German I Air Corps, which was under the command of General P. Deichmann. The above table does not include communication, courier, transport or Hungarian Air Force aircraft.

Soviet peasants and Hungarian pilots on an airfield in Ukraine that has been occupied by an aviation detachment from the MKHL in summer 1941. The fighter that can be seen standing behind them is a CR.42.

Hungarian soldiers from the 'Mobile Corps' at the crash site of a downed Soviet SB bomber.

An Re.2000 fighter, that had belonged to the 1/I V.Osz group, on its way to the Eastern Front in early summer 1942.

A captured Soviet I-15bis fighter at an exhibition in Budapest in June 1942.

A propaganda exhibition in Budapest was aimed at demonstrating to the city's population the successes of the war. An armoured Il-2 ground-attack aircraft inspired a great deal of interest from locals.

An Fi 156 liaison aircraft with Hungarian markings circles over Hungarian Second Army positions.

Hungarian pilots from the 1st Air Brigade, which have been decorated with German Iron Crosses 1st and 2nd Class.

An Re.2000 fighter from Major K. Chukasha's group. Following assimilation of these Italian-made aircraft, Hungarian crews considered them to be amongst the best aircraft types they had at their disposal in summer 1942.

Son of Hungarian regent, Horthy Ishtvan, in the cabin of Re.2000. He died in crash on a training sortie in the Eastern Front on 20 August 1942.

Obsolete German Ju 86K aircraft were used by the Hungarian Air Force in the East predominantly for urgent deliveries of vital spare parts and matériel to combat groups.

Hungarian soldiers in Kiev inspect a heavy German Ju-88C-6 ground-attack aircraft.

The winter of 1942/43 took a heavy toll on Hungarian aviation since it emerged that aircraft had not been prepared for operations in freezing conditions from snow-covered airfields. Whilst just 20 combat sorties were flown in January, almost all the Re.2000 aircraft had to be abandoned or were blown up. Two aircraft are shown on Rossoshi airfield.

Hungarian reconnaissance personnel carried out a very active reconnaissance programme from Kharkov airfield using a Ju 88D from the 1/1 detachment, in particular of the Soviet airfields at Kursk, Svoboda and Kastorniy.

According to historical documents, during January and February 1943, the Hungarian Air Brigade lost 39 aircraft and 170 personnel, including 82 that were considered irrevocable losses. This photograph shows one of the Ar 96 aircraft abandoned on the airfield during the withdrawal.

Raba Botond II truck after Il-2 attack, winter 1943.

A group of Hungarian trucks are moving along the winter road in Voronezh region. The anti-aircraft cannon is on alert position.

A German pilot from KG3 squadron, who had been decorated with the Knight's Cross, passes on the art of aircraft handling and combat skills to his Hungarian ally in the cockpit of a Ju 88.

Hungarian pilots get ready to defend their country from air attacks in spring 1944 with servicing and preparations for a sortie in a Bf109G-6. Almost the entire complement of aircraft had to be recalled from the Eastern Front.

A group of four-engine American Flying Fortress bombers in flight over Hungary.

Hungarians prepare Messerschmitts for a scramble in May 1944.

Hungarian soldiers next to a B-24 of the 459th Squadron, United States 15th Air Force, that was shot down by anti-aircraft artillery on 7 July 1944.

This P-38J long-range escort fighter shot down in aerial combat made an emergency landing in western Hungary on 22 August 1944.

A group of Liberator heavy bombers fly over the outskirts of Szolnok.

One of the Il-4 bombers belonging to the III Main Air Corps on its way to target a railway junction at Budapest.

Hungarian crew of He.111 bomber before a training sortie at Solnok airfield, 1944.

German Ju-88G-6 night fighters from the 5/NJG100 detachment simultaneously repelled night raids by Soviet and English bombers in autumn 1944. Archive documents show this unit fought very successfully on the night of 23 February 1944, claiming five Li-2 aircraft shot down.

The Commander of Long-Range Aviation, Marshal A.E. Golovanov, near his headquarters in the Petrov Palace building in Moscow.

Major N.A. Krapiva from the 27th Guards Hunter-Blocker Regiment fought successfully against German night fighters in Hungary, using the ACAB (Automatic Combined Artillery Battery) gun emplacement.

The commander of the 2nd Ukrainian Front, Marshal of the Soviet Union R.Y. Malinovsky, and member of the Military Council General A.N. Tevchenkov (on the left in the front row) with Heroes of the Soviet Union (infantrymen, sappers, artillerymen and pilots) decorated for their achievements in western Hungary.

2

Combat Drags On – Further Stages of the Offensive

The Red Army's Kecskemét–Budapest offensive came as a surprise to the Germans. On 31 October, two days after the launch of the operation, the Military Council of the 2nd Ukrainian Front sent a plan for the continuation of the offensive to Stalin in Moscow, comprising the reinforcement of the main assault group and making use of reserves: "Thus, this Plan implies that 36 rifle divisions, three cavalry corps and four tank corps will be fighting between the Danube River and the Tisza River from 10 November 1944." These formations were expected to be supported not only by the 5th Air Army, but also by the principal forces of the 17th Air Army. The following day, the Soviet First Deputy Chief of General Staff, General of the Army A.I. Antonov, telegraphed 2nd Ukrainian Front commander Marshal Malinovsky to inform him: "The Supreme Commander-in-Chief authorized the redeployment of the 6th Guards Tank Army and Group Pliyev in the direction of Budapest [and ordered that] the planning of the offensive in terms of dates and objectives be reported [to Moscow] before 3 November."

In early November, the Germans strove to eliminate the penetration of Soviet troops towards Budapest at all costs. To do so, they promptly redeployed three tank divisions and a motorized division from Miskolc and halted the advance of the 46th Army. In response, Malinovsky decided to shift the main assault to the sector of the 7th Guards Army and ordered General I.A. Pliyev's Cavalry Mechanized Group to attack from the Szolnok area to the north, along the west bank of the Tisza River. Two Guards Mechanized Corps were also carrying out operations in this area. Without ceasing active operations, the Soviet forces, throughout the first 10 days of November, carried out intense preparations for a decisive attack on the German and Hungarian troops defending the south-east of Budapest.

The Red Air Force was quite active on several occasions during this time. For example, on 1 November, Goryunov's 5th Air Army pilots performed 621 combat sorties (507 crews flew, in total, 748 hours and 31 minutes): A-20Gs made 67 sorties; Pe-2s made six sorties (for long-range reconnaissance purposes); Il-2s made 174 sorties; La-45s made 135 sorties; Yak-1s and Yak-9s together made 182 sorties; and Po-2s made 57 sorties (during the previous night). According to the crews' reports, this resulted in the destruction of 69 motor vehicles, 25 railway troop trains, two steam locomotives, 12 carriages with various cargoes and two ammunition depots. Furthermore, fire from eight Axis anti-aircraft attack batteries and one field artillery battery were suppressed, 13 seats of fire were initiated and eight explosions were noted. Their opponents, in groups of eight to 12 FW 190s, attempted to deliver strikes on Soviet troop formations and to counteract combat operations of the Red Air Force. According to Soviet pilots' reports, clashes with the enemy resulted in bringing down 17 of their aircraft, with two Bf 109s credited to the Bostons' gunners. Repofrted Soviet combat losses totaled two Yak-1s and an Il-2 (the latter brought down by anti-aircraft fire), while a La-5 and two A-20Gs were hit but managed to land safely.

After several days of respite brought about by poor weather, on 5 November airmen of the 5th Air Army flew 482 combat sorties, but this was followed by another brief hiatus. Then on 8 November, 590 sorties were made, when without incurring any losses, the Soviet pilots intercepted and downed two He 111s in the fog. According to the Operations Record Book of the 5th Air Army for 10 November, "Units of the Air Army performed no operations on account of bad weather conditions and soaked aerodromes." It was also emphasized that no flyovers by enemy aircraft had been registered, but that maintenance personnel had worked to enhance the serviceability of aircraft, 19 crews from the 149th Guards Fighter Regiment had been transferred to the town of Kocser and 16 crews of the 177th Guards Fighter Regiment were redeployed to the banks of the Tisza.

On 13 November, the Soviet crews flew a total of 702 sorties (to which the German-Hungarian air forces responded with 425 flyovers), with a focus on attacking ground targets. According to reports by the crews, the operations resulted in the destruction of four enemy tanks, a steam locomotive and 32 dray-carts, and in the suppression of fire of three field artillery batteries, three anti-aircraft batteries and five Oerlikon batteries. In 21 sorties, Soviet pilots reported downing 26 enemy aircraft, including 15 Bf 109s. The list of claimed victories included a Bf 110 (which was actually not employed by the Germans in the theater of operations) and two Ju 88s (although the *Luftwaffe* actually flew only Ju 188s, which bore an external resemblance to Ju 88s, using them as long-range reconnaissance aircraft, and no relevant losses or damage were reported). According to German documents, the claimed efficiency of these Soviet operations seem considerably exaggerated.

However, the Hungarian Air Force had at its disposal two-engined multipurpose Bf 110s and Me 210s (which bore a considerable resemblance to the Bf 110). The Me 210s were not widely used by the *Luftwaffe*, but Hungarian crews liked the aircraft, and during the autumn of 1944 they frequently clashed with Soviet aircraft. The Hungarian 102nd Group of high-speed bombers (*102 G.B.Oz.*) engaged in combat in early November 1944; on 13 November, six Me 210s from the *102/2* unit was dive-bombing Soviet positions to the east of Budapest, along the Újszász–Jászberény road. An aircraft bearing the serial Z-116 was damaged by anti-aircraft fire, and finally brought down by a La-5 (the 12th personal victory credited to Senior Lieutenant A.D. Dogadailo of the 177th Guards Fighter Regiment). The Hungarian aircraft crashed to the north-west of Heves, and the crew, under *Oberleutnant* G. Halmay, were killed. According to the Hungarians, one of the 102nd Group's most experienced pilots, *Oberfeldwebel* J. Orban, downed two Soviet fighters in aerial combat on 13 November.

Following a detailed reconnaissance (largely performed by the *NAGr14* short-range reconnaissance group), the Germans would have a clear idea of Soviet plans, which were to capture the city and strongpoint of Hatvan. The Operations Report of 14 November by the German Sixth Army, which was defending the approaches to Budapest, to the Army Group South Headquarters stated that the Red Army "with strong support from aviation was pursuing the offensive. It turned out, also, that the enemy was planning an advance in the west direction until they reach the Koka area. Both motorized units of the enemy [the II and IV Mechanized Corps] were advancing from the eastern flank in a north-westerly direction to Jászdózsa." Principal air operations on the Soviet side (mainly sorties made by ground-attack aircraft of Stepichev's II Attack Corps) were noted in the sector of the German LVII Panzer Corps.

The 16 November report of the German Sixth Army Headquarters put extreme emphasis on the air situation:

> The greater part of the enemy's aircraft were acting above the sector of the LVII Panzer Corps. There are large quantities of bomber aircraft [usually Il-2s and Bostons, although sometimes La-5s carried out bombing and strike attacks too] performing their missions under fighter cover. The German–Hungarian air forces employed 420 aircraft to support defensive battles of our troops near Lány and Jászárokszállás. Twenty-eight aircraft of the enemy were brought down, and seven tanks were knocked out. The 4th Anti-Aircraft Regiment [commanded by Colonel F. von Arnim] downed two enemy aircraft.

In Soviet reports, however, the very same events were presented in a different light as follows:

> The 5th Air Army performed 535 combat sorties. Thirty-six enemy aircraft were downed in air battles [these successes were greatly exaggerated]. The enemy's air force, in groups of 10 to 30 aircraft, were bombing the combat formations of the 7th Guards Army and the 46th Army, Pliyev's groups, the II Guards Mechanized Corps and the IV Guards Mechanized Corps. [The *SG10* wing performed highly intensive operations within this sector; in spite of the bad weather, many German pilots flew three sorties each.] In total, 300 aircraft flyovers were recorded. Our anti-aircraft artillery shot down four enemy aircraft. [Soviet losses were not reported].

Soviet documents indicate that although weather conditions remained difficult, the greatest intensity of sorties by both the Soviet and German–Hungarian air forces were reported during the period from 13–17 November, when a Soviet offensive to Hatvan and Gyöngyös was launched to envelop Budapest from the north-east. Staff officers of the 5th Air Army noted that unlike previous air combats in Hungary, the enemy's fighters were now considerably more active, with Bf 109s covering ground-attack aircraft FW 190s and Ju 87s, and with fighter-bomber Bf 110s and Me 210s. They were repeatedly patrolling the flight routes of Soviet bombers; this was erroneously attributed by Soviet officers to the arrival of the *JG3* Udet fighter-wing in the sector.

It should be noted that German losses in air combats would have been greater if the Red Army Air Force pilots had conducted aerial battles in a more active manner. Even the most experienced and well-trained air warriors, the 'Stalin's Falcons', flew most sorties in large formations; as a result, they were constrained and unable to fully realize their potential. Thus, for example, one of the best fighter aces of the III Guards Fighter Corps, Hero of the Soviet Union Captain K.A. Yevstigneyev, flew 32 combat sorties during the period from mid-October 1944 to mid-January 1945. Of these, 25 sorties were to cover Soviet troops on the battlefield, two were for reconnaissance, three to escort ground-attack and bomber aircraft, and only two sorties were for 'free hunting'. During this time, Yevstigneyev downed two FW 190s and a Bf 109 in 17 air combats, but undoubtedly he could have achieved far greater success if he had been given more freedom of operation. It is possible, however, that this outstanding fighter pilot was granted some rest after the intense battles of the summer of 1944.

The report of the III Guards Fighter Corps Staff mentions that many talented pilots were inhibited by the strict limitations of their missions. On the rare occasions when 'free hunting' mission sorties were performed, their efficiency was low, due to an absence of systematic surveillance of German aerodromes in Hungary, lack of perseverance in the course of pre-reconnaissance and poor knowledge of the most preferable flight courses and altitudes. Analyzing the results of the battles in November, Deputy Corps Commander General A.S. Prostoserdov pointed out: "Today it is a shame to come back from 'hunting' without success. Therefore, you must carefully watch the enemy and study its habits."

German and Hungarian crews, on the contrary, persevered in their air reconnaissance and penetrated deep into the Soviet rear area, to the western regions of Romania and Bulgaria. On at least three occasions, Axis bombers, having studied their enemy's work schedule and air defense systems, delivered strikes on Soviet aerodromes in Hungary. Records show that twice in the course of the current operation, they "destroyed Békéscsaba during the period of tanks unloading, and bombed Arad thrice with our troops concentrated there". All these targets were located in western Hungary, which had been liberated shortly before. Traffic was also attacked on the road between Timişoara to Oradea in eastern Romania.

As far as cover for the Soviet's main attacking force was concerned, the front line in November was not always clearly defined and anti-aircraft artillery was lagging behind. Groups of up to six FW 190s attacked roads and bridges from a height of 300–400m, sometimes even descending to treetop height. Well-armed and armored Focke-Wulfs avoided engaging with Soviet fighters. Instead, they usually emerged from behind mountains or hills, then disappeared close to ground level using folds in the terrain. Intercepts by Soviet aircraft were rarely successful, and German losses were mostly caused by fire from the ground. The Soviets' difficulties can be seen in the memoirs of the Deputy Commander of the 6th Guards Fighter Division, Lieutenant Colonel B.N. Yeremin, whose unit initially ensured the security of the 53rd Army troops and later the Cavalry Mechanized Group Pliyev:

> Initially, the troops were moving in a compact mass; in such cases we fighters can rather easily provide cover from the air. But then the attacking troops entered the mountainous and forest areas and split into several directions over the rather wide front ... This march along the soaked autumn roads for a long time afterwards lingered in my memory. We had no special-purpose radio stations mounted on off-road vehicles; sophisticated radio equipment was mounted on ordinary trucks. Our radio station was mounted on a Studebaker; but those soaked roads were not good enough even for tracked vehicles, let alone a Studebaker.

General Prostoserdov also commented on the Soviet radio problems:

> The radar stations are not used in a proper way. They failed to become a powerful aid for division commanders and staff officers in the fighting of the airborne adversary. According to Redoute [Soviet radar] data, the number of mission sorties is small, considerably less than upon a call from the Observation Post. And it should be vice versa. And the fighters' arrival upon a call from the Observation Post is almost always late, because of large distances. We have to make maximal use of Redoute, without fearing that a sortie will involve no encounters with the enemy's aircraft.

The III Guards Fighter Corps command drew the attention of flight crews and commanders to cases of losses in flight during a sortie, especially on the way back from a sortie, which was partially accounted for by an unduly complacent mood. Thus, for example, one of the most efficient Soviet fighter aces in the Hungarian theatre, Lieutenant P.Y. Mordukhovich of the 177th Guards Fighter Regiment (credited with eight personal victories in October, among them a downed Fi 156 communication aircraft of the German Sixth Army Headquarters), was reported missing after a combat sortie on the last day of October. None of his regimental colleagues could say what had happened to him, where the other pilots had been at the moment of his disappearance and why they had failed to provide cover for their fellow group member.

The Germans, meanwhile, paid particular attention to 'free hunting', which constituted the basis of combat operations for entire fighter groups such as *II/JG52*. Such activities were often successful for the Germans, and the Soviets lost many experienced crews as a result of 'surprise' attacks. In the III Guards Fighter Corps, nine pilots were killed between 20 October and 20 November; four of them were from the 178th Guards Fighter Regiment of Captain Yevstigneyev. The regiment lost two Heroes of the Soviet Union: Head of the Military Rifle Service, Captain F.G. Semyonov, and Deputy Squadron Commander, Senior Lieutenant B.V. Zhigulenkov. The latter was most likely killed in a battle with Hungarian air forces, who had considerably intensified their operations.

Available data from Soviet and German sources help to reconstruct what happened in one encounter near midday on 16 November, when five La-5s headed by Captain Yevstigneyev flew in a two-tier formation and then engaged with 12 FW 190s and eight Bf 109s. At the end of their cover time, the group of Lavochkin aircraft first met, near Pusta-Mănăştur, five Messerschmitts flying 1,000m higher than the Soviet aircraft. The Messerschmitts, using their positional advantage, began to attack in pairs. The La-5 fighters attempted luring their opponents over Soviet-held territory, when suddenly a sixth Bf 109 appeared and descended upon the aircraft of Senior Lieutenant B.V. Zhigulenkov, which was hanging behind.

According to Hungarian sources, the lethal attack was undertaken by a Hungarian fighter ace, G. Debrody. During a daytime sortie, he had already brought down a La-5 90km north-east of Budapest; to this, he added another victory by attacking the solitary Lavochkin at close range approximately 50km east of the capital. Captain Yevstigneyev noticed Debrody's Messerschmitt and started turning in his direction, but he was unable to intervene in time. The Bf 109G-6 fired a long burst, then descended abruptly and flew off to the north-west. The starboard wing panel of Zhigulenkov's La-5FN (S/N 39212952) fell off, and the aircraft crashed to thr ground east of the town of Besenzeg; the pilot was killed by a shell burst to the head.

Debrody's fighter was apparently fitted with a 30mm cannon, as evidenced by the type of damage to the Soviet aircraft which he shot down. Hungary's second-best fighter ace, he was credited with 28 victories, but was himself wounded in the stomach, being fired on by Senior Lieutenant P.R. Shchetinin of the 178th Guards Fighter Regiment. Debrody made a forced landing 45km north-east of Budapest and was unable to fly again during the war; his 204th combat sortie turned out to be his last one. For Boris Zhigulenkov, his final combat sortie was his 232nd, during which he had shot down 20 enemy aircraft. His death was said to have been principally caused by a lack of circumspection within the group when away from the front line. The interim commander of the III Guards Fighter Corps, General Prostoserdov, pointed out that a battle formation on a combat sortie should only consist of pairs, and that a Hero of the Soviet Union should fly combat sorties only with an experienced wingman.

Turning to operations conducted by the *II/JG52* (the strongest *Luftwaffe* group) in November 1944, with 28 Bf 109G-6s and 109G-14s at the end of this period and replenished later with 11 new aircraft (among them, fighters fitted with 30mm cannons), this unit claimed 73 downed Soviet aircraft (approximately every second victory claim was confirmed) for the loss of eight of its own aircraft, for various reasons. Six pilots became incapacitated, with three of them killed and three wounded. One of the unit's fighter aces, *Leutnant* P. Düttmann, was twice mentioned in documents during the month. He was injured on 1 November during a landing at the Budapest-Ferihegy aerodrome when his Messerschmitt struck another aircraft. Then on 13 November, sometime after after midday, he was shot down by an Ilyshin Il-2 ground-attack aircraft, parachuted from his stricken aircraft behind the front line, but in spite of his injuries, managed to get back to the German lines. He subsequently spent many weeks in hospital. Meanwhile, young *Leutnant* H. Ewald claimed 10 victories and proved to be one of the most efficient pilots during November; by the end of the month, his score reached 42. The results of the leading fighter aces who contributed to success are provided in the table below.

As for the Hungarian aviatiors, the *101 V.Ez.* fighter group performed 80 combat sorties against the English and American air forces and 157 combat sorties against the Soviets during November 1944. Their most intense and successful day in combat was 16 November, with 14 victories scored. However, the Hungarians were generally losing one of their aircraft for each victory achieved. The most successful of the Hungarian fighter aces was *Oberfeldwebel* I. Fabian, who claimed three downed aircraft during the month. The Hungarian casualties included 11 pilots killed (among them Squadron Commander *Oberleutnant* B. Fulecky and *Kapitän* G. Michna, who had seven victories), two missing and five wounded. For the bombers of *102 G.B.Oz.*, the most important sorties were those attacking the Danube crossings or concentrations of troops on both banks, when their losses were less than those among the single-engined fighters.

Many Soviet documents recognize the good average level of training of their enemy's flight crews, as well as the considerable Soviet losses. Thus, for example, the report by the Red Army Air Force Headquarters for November 1944 placed an emphasis on the high intensity of battles over Hungary and the strength of the enemy's two-tier or three-tier patrols: "Throughout the past month, aircraft of the 5th Air Army and the 17th Air Army encountered considerable resistance on the part of the enemy fighters during combat operations. For example, of 131 air battles fought by our pilots in November all over the Soviet–German Front, 102 battles were fought by units under the command of General S.K. Goryunov and V.A. Sudets."

The Soviet offensive developed throughout Hungary. The German command could see that the Soviets were about to enter the flatlands near Budapest and to capture bridgeheads on the western bank of the Danube. Timely redeployment of its air forces enabled the Red Army Air Force to operate actively and to provide efficient support to the attacking Soviet motorized units. The German command had managed to restore the front after the collapse in Romania, but the situation remained critical for Army Group South; aircraft of the I Air Corps, which was supporting the troops in Hungary, were making strenuous efforts to stem the Soviet tide. One of the best German dive-bomber pilots in the theatre, Commodore of the Immelmann Wing H.-U. Rudel, recalled those days:

> The Russians manage to occupy the aerodromes around Debrecen, and we now have to fight an enemy that exceeds us in number several times. Meanwhile, we keep suffering losses from anti-aircraft fire and have problems with supplies, whereas the replacements leave much to be desired. Still, the Soviets cannot take the entire credit for our hardships; they have to thank their Western allies whose strategic bombers considerably upset the operation of our communications by constantly delivering strikes on cities and railway stations. To cap the defeat, there are American fighter-bombers, which keep sneaking above the railway lines. We are just unable to protect our communications for lack of people and equipment.
>
> My wing has only a few aircraft left, including those of the anti-tank unit [at the beginning of October, Rudel's wing actually had at its disposal 50 Focke-Wulfs (mostly F-8s), 30 Ju 87D-5s dive bombers and 13 Ju 87G-2 anti-tank aircraft; approximately half of them were operable.]. Nevertheless, we often perform combat sorties to the Kecskemét area. Our air forces are so weak that once I had to fly alone to attack the enemy tanks with an escort of four FW 190s. Approaching Kecskemét, I hardly believed my eyes: There was an endless column of Soviet tanks moving along the road to the north of the city. Above the tanks,

Ace	Victories total as of 31 October 1944	Victories total as of 30 November 1944	Results for November	Remark
Kapitän E. Hartmann	306	327	21	
Major G. Barkhorn	274	285	11	
Oberleutnant H. Lipfert	152	158	6	
Leutnant P. Düttmann	118	127	9	Wounded in battle
Kapitän H. Sturm	116	119	3	

a whole swarm of fighters were hanging like a cluster of grapes, covering the attack group.

In attacks on combat formations of Soviet troops, German bombers and ground-attack aircraft approached the target area in a wedge formation or in a column of six formation, then they re-formed. The He 111s bombed in a shallow descent (usually from an altitude of 1,500–2,500m, depending on anti-aircraft fire conditions), whereas the Ju 87s dived from altitudes of 2,500–4,000m and dropped their bombs from under the cloud base. Meanwhile, the FW 190 s approached in groups of four to nine aircraft (sometimes, a group might contain up to 35 aircraft) at an altitude of 1,000–3,000m in nine-strong column or wedge formations. The German bombers approached either from territory controlled by Soviet troops or from out of the sun . In the target area, the group assumed an echelon formation, and the aircraft performed bombing runs in a dive at an angle of up to 60°, usually in one pass. After releasing the bombs, the Focke-Wulfs descended and attacked the targets with gun- and cannon-fire, in three or four passes until their ammunition was exhausted. During the strafing attack, approximately one-third of the group remained in the upper tier to cover the other aircraft in case Soviet fighters appeared.

If the Soviet fighters did appear, the FW 190 ground-attack aircraft promptly released their bombs, reformed into a defensive circle and tried to lure the Soviet aircraft over German-held territory and, where possible, into German anti-aircraft fire. There were occasions when aircraft of *SG2* and *SG10* wings, upon encountering Soviet ground-attack aircraft, immediately dropped their bombs and launched an attack, in order to prevent precision strikes by the Ilyushin aircraft on the German combat formations on the ground and, if possible, bring down one or two aircraft into the bargain.

The first stage of the Budapest offensive ended on 28 November. Two days before, the commander of the 2nd Ukrainian Front, Marshal R.Y. Malinovsky, suspended active operations in order to carry out a redeployment. Communication lines were too stretched, the roads soaked, and it took time to move up fresh reserves. The intention was to encircle and eliminate Axis forces defending Budapest. Approximately a month after the beginning of the Red Army's offensive in Hungary, the enemy's defenses had been breached between the Tisza and the Danube, and Soviet forces had advanced north-west up to 100km, thereby providing the preconditions for future success.

The summary report by the *Wehrmacht* Supreme Command of 29 November 1944, however, provided quite a positive evaluation of Army Group South's defensive actions:

> In battles in Central Hungary between Budapest and Miskolc, our forces quelled the enemy's attempt to capture Budapest by a strike from the south-east and to break through to western Hungary along the borderline with Slovakia. The German troops together with our Hungarian allies, under the general command of Colonel General J. Friessner, held back the almost incessant, from 29 October, surge of 61 divisions and seven tank corps of the Bolsheviks and the Romanians. The enemy suffered heavy personnel and matériel losses.

If we compare the number of aircraft in the Soviet 5th Air Army at the beginning of November with those at the end of the month, we can conclude that in spite of inputs and replacements, the number decreased by 50. Ground-attack aircraft suffered serious damage, both in air battles and from anti-aircraft fire. In the III Guards Corps and V Attack Corps there had been 300 Il-2s, but only 227 had survived, and approximately a quarter of those aircraft needed repairing. On the other hand, the 17th Air Army had previously only been deploying in the area and mainly supporting the 57th Army, but by the end of November it was supporting troops of the 3rd Ukrainian Front in battles for footholds on the west bank of the Danube.

During October and early November, the 17th Air Army had conducted operations in Yugoslavia together with units of the National Liberation Army of Yugoslavia, provided cover for Belgrade and rendered immense assistance to the Yugoslavs in the creation of their own air force. Members of the 17th Air Army were assigned as instructors and training pilots, and training centers were arranged to train pilots, navigators, radio operators, gunners, engineers and technicians. The greatest assistance to Yugoslavia was provided by the air group under the command of General A.N. Vitruk. However, the 17th Air Army then started redeploying to Hungary to support the offensive of the 3rd Ukrainian Front.

The situation seemed to be developing favorably for the Soviets. Furthermore, bombers of the Western Allies kept on attacking important targets all across Hungary, inflicting heavy casualties on the German–Hungarian anti-aircraft forces. Fighter-bombers, which repeatedly caught aircraft unawares parked on aerodromes and destroyed hundreds of pieces of rolling-stock, were just as dangerous. For example, a surprise attack by Mustangs near Lake Balaton on 6 November resulted in the loss to *II/JG51* of two flying aces, *Leutnant* K. Hammer and *Leutnant* H. Sieckenius, who were both killed in their Messerschmitts.

At the time, several high-ranking followers of Hungarian Regent M. Horthy, on receipt of the news of the Szálasi coup and aware of the sentiments of generals and senior officers, went over to the Red Army. The former Chief of the General Staff, Colonel General J. Vörös, along with providing most valuable information on events in his country, volunteered to help take Hungary out of the war. On 7 November, General Staff Colonel Hatzegy, who at the time held the position of Chief of Staff for the Hungarian VII Army Corps, used a Fieseler Fi 156 Storch aircraft to fly across the front line and desert to the Soviets; he took with him several valuable documents and maps indicating the location of ammunition depots, radio stations, major concentrations of forces and – what was of the greatest importance – the best places for troops to cross the Danube.

Meantime, Soviet forces also experienced several tragic incidents, the most notorious of which occurred on 7 November. Near the Yugoslavian town of Nish, a column of troops of the 37th Army suffered a bombing and strike attack by US Lockheed P-38 Lightnings, which mistook the Soviet troops for Germans. When the situation was reported to 17th Air Army commander General Sudets, he ordered an immediate halt to the attack; but how was this to be done? The situation was saved by Captain A.I. Koldunov of the 866th Fighter Regiment, who started off, at the head of eight Yakovlev aircraft, for the area where the Soviet columns were marching. The Americans were meanwhile ready to deliver a strike on a Soviet aerodrome. It seemed that the Soviet fighters would be too late. An eyewitness of the situation, Colonel B.A. Smirnov, who was then in command of the 288th Fighter Division (to which the 866th Regiment belonged), recalled:

> Meanwhile two American groups, 25 to 30 aircraft in each, were approaching the west edge of the aerodrome. The upper group formed a circle and was getting ready to cover the lower group. The lower group split into two more equal subgroups. One of them started assaulting a column of our troops on the road by subjecting it to gun and cannon fire from low altitude; the other one was attacking the taking-off fighters. As a result, four American Lightning fighters were brought down (one of them was downed by anti-aircraft gunners). We lost two crews. Lieutenant D.P. Krivonogikh and Junior Lieutenant V.M. Shipulin were killed in action. Lieutenant A.M. Zhestovsky's aircraft was hit, and the pilot bailed out ... During the assault, the Commander of the VI Guards Corps, General G.P. Kotov, was killed by the Americans.

Documents reveal that throughout the day, the 17th Air Army performed 131 combat sorties (119 of them during daylight). In eight of these missions, Soviet Yak-9s endeavored to intercept the Americans who had lost their bearings:

> The Soviet fighters were conducting the battle for self-defense purposes [Junior Lieutenant Shipulin's Lightning was shot down by Soviet anti-aircraft gunners, and the American pilot burned to death in his cockpit] trying to show to the Americans that the latter were mistaken. Thanks to the resolute actions of the Hero of the Soviet Union Captain A.I. Koldunov, who approached the lead aircraft of the Lightning group and pointed to the Soviet insignia with his hand, the Americans stopped the assault; the battle was over.

The situation was heating up by the minute. Captain Koldunov made an abrupt maneuver and showed up behind an American. However, Koldunov did not open fire; instead, in an instant, he forced the wingman out of the way and came as close as possible to the American commander. The Lightnings could not fire because they feared that they might hit their own lead aircraft. The Americans then understood their mistake and ceased firing. Following an investigation into the incident, an American representative apologized to the Front Command for what had happened and expressed condolences in respect of the dead. He explained that the leader of the Lighnings had lost his bearings and mistaken the column of Soviet troops for a German one. Koldunov, who had demonstrated courage and initiative to avert further loss of life in the action, was awarded the Order of the Red Banner.

Nine November brought important events for the 3rd Ukrainian Front. On that day, Front commander Marshal F.I. Tolbukhin ordered the speeding up of repairs to ships and for the Danube Military Flotilla to start minesweeping the river's navigable channels. He also demanded that the Flotilla be ready to render assistance in the near future to the troops of the 57th Army and 4th Guards Army along the Danube to the north of the mouth of the Drava River. In view of the need to perform an assault landing in the course of the attack on Budapest which was being prepared, the Front Command asked the *Stavka* to provide an additional separate brigade of the Black Sea Fleet Marines. On the same day, the Apatin-Kaposvár offensive was launched. During the night of 8/9 November, units of the LXXV Rifle Corps (of the 57th Army) successfully completed an offensive reconnaissance operation near Batina, and two companies crossed the Danube to secure two small bridgeheads on the opposite bank.

During the succeeding four nights, the principal forces of two divisions crossed the river under fire and bombing from German forces. Fierce battles continued by day and night, and units of the Soviet corps suffered heavy losses. "The way to the west was again barred by a wide water obstacle, again the Danube, which soon after the confluence with the Sava made a turn to the north," a report of the LXXV Rifle Corps stated. "Thus the troops of the 57th Army had to force-cross the Danube again. Crossing the river at the exit from Serbia turned out to be much more difficult than at the entrance to the country. On the other side of the river mouth, in the enemy's rear, there were no operative Resistance units this time, and the populace was hostile."

Here, on both sides of the river, the Yugoslavs were fighting together with Soviet troops. In attempts to drive the defenders of the Batina bridgehead back into the Danube, the German command began to use armored vehicles and large numbers of German, Hungarian and also Croatian forces, with combat groups committed to battle against the Soviet positions. The Batina area witnessed many sorties by the *Luftwaffe* (night ground-attack aircraft being especially active), which had been mostly idle during the Belgrade offensive. It was later discovered that a German radio station was operating in the Soviet troops' rear in a cemetery near the village of Bezdan, being used to direct the German aircraft onto Soviet targets. This was located and eliminated only after several days of battles.

On 17 November, the first combat sortie was performed by the Romanian 2nd Air Group, which had been redeployed at the beginning of the month to the Turkeve aerodrome in Hungary, to the east of Szolnok. The group, replenished with IAR.81C aircraft, carried out a strafing attack and was credited with destroying a truck in an Axis column. On the same day, a solitary Romanian Ju 87 (most probably, other aircraft had failed to join it due to technical problems) flew without cover to attack the positions of the Hungarian Third Army to the south of Budapest. The aircraft was soon intercepted by Messerschmitts and severely damaged, with the pilot also wounded. However, the appearance of Romanian fighters sidetracked the Germans' attention, and Adjunct N. Stan managed to land his stricken aircraft at one of the Soviet aerodromes. After landing, he lost consciousness, but Soviet medics saved the pilot's life, and he saw out the end of the war in hospital.

Up until mid-November, Sudets' 17th Air Army had only made infrequent sorties, but it then rendered stronger support to the neighboring 5th Air Army. For example, on 20 November, when the 5th Air Army's aerodrome was blanketed with fog and its units were grounded, the 17th Air Army supported the attack on Batina and Apatin. Sudets' crews undertook bombing and strike attacks against German troops, and a group of 24 aircraft delivered a strike on the Axis aerodrome at Pécs (in total, 647 combat sorties were made that day). The Germans counteracted fiercely, claiming eight destroyed Soviet aircraft. According to German sources, five victories were credited to strafing attacks by the *SG10* wing; of these, two Lavochkin aircraft were shot down by *Oberleutnant* H. Pohl to open his operational record in Hungary.

According to a summary report, the 17th Air Army had 1,031 aircraft at its disposal at the end of November. To use these forces to maximum benefit, the aircraft had to be operated as close to the forward combat troops as possible, but the muddy season caused serious difficulties in redeployment. All aerodromes' runways were saturated, meaning armoured forces could receive no aerial support. The situation had to be resolved, and Sudets ordered the preparation of runways near the Danube where sandy ground offered improved drainage. Consequently, Deputy Commander for Aviation Engineering Service of the 10thAttack Corps, Engineer Colonel V.A. Baranovich, oversaw the laying down of log decking covered with metal sheets to provide an all-weather runway.

The Soviets' Il-2s could now take off from the makeshift aerodromes using thrust-augmentation techniques. The situation was outlined in a report by their Aviation Engineering Service:

> To ferry the aircraft to another aerodrome, a take-off runway was constructed. It was essentially a wooden decking 15m wide and 300m long. The wooden decking [made from logs] was topped with sand, crushed stone and slag. The runway had very limited parameters; therefore, the ferry flights were made only by experienced flight crews. Take-off was performed on aircraft with reduced weight. Besides, forward of the runway, all trees were hewn for a distance of 200m. Two days after the construction of the runway, the required regiment was ferried to a new location.

One of the leading fighter aces of the 17th Air Army, N.M. Skomorokhov of the 31st Fighter Regiment, recalled the move to a floodplain meadow near the village of Madosca on the banks of the Danube:

> The village itself stood on a hill, and the aerodrome was located in lowland. It was damp and insecure. Our wing was the first to land here ... Only a few people had by that time arrived from the air-base service squadron; we had ourselves to redeploy the aircraft and to station the sentries. None of the local residents appeared, and we found an ancient empty building with 1m-thick walls for the overnight accommodation. At about 2 o'clock at night, we were roused by a firefight somewhere nearby. We grappled our guns and got ready to fight. Then I saw some trucks driving up to our house, with armed people sitting in the truck beds. The people jumped down to the ground and began making roll-ups and lighting them using flint and steel to have a smoke. This 'old-fashioned' technique to strike fire was at the time employed only by Soviet soldiers. So we understood that these people were friends not foes.

The most technically advanced redeployment technique was to make use of transport aircraft, which allowed redeploying of technical personnel in a quick and 'compact' manner and to start normal preparation for combat operations on the day of the move. However, during this offensive operation, the Lisunov Li-2s transports were not used for this purpose. As for motor vehicles, if provided, their quantity was insufficient and they were worn out. As a result, the redeployment was taking longer than intended. By the time the technical personnel arrived, as they used to put it, at a 'new base point', the air unit had already moved off to another location. Thus, with rather frequent redeployment of air units from one aerodrome to another, which often was the case in 1944, technical personnel and air gunners were constantly on the move and could not take part in combat operations. The number of redeployments also affected the condition of matériel at the base points.

Many unusual situations occurred in the course of these redeployments of air units and detachments. For example, Senior Technician Lieutenant P.M. Vyunin and Senior Technician Lieutenant M.A. Myakota of the 295th Fighter Division chose to take charge of the disassembling of their aircraft. They removed the wing panels and landing gear doors and placed the fuselage tail units in GAZ-MM or GAZ-AA trucks (which had a capacity of 1.5 tons), then the mechanic personnel headed by Technician Lieutenant V.D. Sokolov arranged the safe towing of aircraft by road. Thirty La-5 fighters were also taken to Baja under their own power along unpaved roads for a distance of 60km; it was later found that 44 tires and 13 air tubes were damaged to such an extent that they were unserviceable. Along with replacing the tires and air tubes, technical personnel had to inspect and clean all surfaces, which were caked in mud. However, an attempt to thus redeploy Il-2 ground-attack aircraft failed because the aircraft were too big to be transported by road, and neither could they take off because of soaked aerodromes; consequently, the ground-attack units were lagging behind the advance.

According to the memoirs of pilot Grigory Sivkov of the 210th Attack Regiment (10thAttack Corps), who, like N.M. Skomorokhov, later twice became a Hero of the Soviet Union, the first half of the autumn was a quiet and informative time, though the on-going war sometimes manifested itself. Sivkov said his ground-attack group made only one sortie from their Belgrade aerodrome to perform reconnaissance and photographing, while among the interesting things that happened was a meeting with a US Lockheed P-38 which had mistakenly landed at the aerodrome. He also noted the generally amiable attitude of the local residents. However, he continued:

> Then we flew to Hungary and occupied an aerodrome near the town of Szeged. Our fighters had already arrived there. Suddenly enemy planes attacked the aerodrome. Our fighters took off promptly. They drove away the enemy; one of the 'Messers' was shot down. Ivan Grigoryev was wounded and sent to the hospital. In a week, however, he rejoined the unit, in spite of having to walk with a stick.
>
> The Hungarian population met us warmly. There was no inhospitality or coldness in the eyes of the Hungarians. On the contrary, their faces were lit with amiability and curiosity. Our smart guys, gunners and motormen, grew accustomed quite quickly, and, in spite of the totally strange Hungarian language, soon held lively conversations with the Hungarians. It is not difficult, of course, to learn a dozen or two words. Just add expressive gestures, and the communication will be all right, if both sides are willing to communicate.
>
> The aerodrome accommodated two regiments; a fighter regiment and an attack regiment. [As far as is known, along with the 210th Attack Regiment there was the 164th Fighter Regiment under Lieutenant Colonel A.D. Melentyev.] They helped each other in all possible ways, with deed or advice. In other words, they were living like two Soviet families abroad. The fighters were located on one side of the runway, and the ground-attack aircraft were arranged on the other side. Major A.L. Kondratkov [commander of the 230th Attack Regiment] held an informal meeting with the technical personnel and ordered, 'Everything should be in perfect order! We are not at home and should behave accordingly. Is it clear?'
>
> Of course, it was clear to everybody without any instructions. Our technicians, young men and girls, spent days and nights on duty near the aircraft, had nearly no rest at all. The aircraft were kept ready for combat. One morning, when the weather was not fit for flying, the technicians were carrying out trial runs of the engines and checking the aircraft for readiness. Everything was all right. Suddenly they saw a fighter making a turn on the opposite side of the runway and running in a strange manner in circles. And the technicians from the neighboring regiment were running after it. Our wing's technician Nikolai Stupin understood at once that something was wrong; he jumped onto the fighter's wing, got to the cockpit, and stopped the aircraft. Later we found out that the technician from the neighboring regiment had been preparing the aircraft for engine starting. There had been nobody nearby to open the air bottle. So he had got out of the cockpit, opened the valve of the compressed air bottle, and the engine had started at once. The aircraft had leaped, jumped over the wheel chocks, torn off the pipe, and started playing tricks on the runway. Luckily, Stupin intervened. So the Regiment Commander awarded him a commendation.

Technician Lieutenant N.V. Stupin received the third State Award, the Order of the Patriotic War 2nd class, for his prompt actions. The recommendation stated that Stupin, who had been in the Red Army since 1936 and in the lines since July 1941, had in November that year been posted to the 210th Attack Regiment, where he had risen from Junior Specialist to Senior Unit Technician. In total, together with his unit, he arranged 294 combat sorties of Il-2s without a single failure through the fault of the technical personnel. The recommendation recorded that "under his direct supervision, the unit repaired 95 aircraft and 30 engines and replaced two engines". Throughout the previous month of military activities, Stupin had "put three young mechanics from the replacement forces in service and taught them to competently carry out maintenance of the Il-2 aircraft with AM-38f engine".

Marshal Rodion Malinovskiy led the Soviet forces that entered Hungarian territory at the end of September 1944. They were faced with the task of driving all Axis forces out of the country.

Colonel General Johannes Friessner commanded the German Army Group South up until the end of December 1944, after which he was removed from his post by the Führer for his failures in Hungary.

Hero of the Soviet Union Captain A.A. Golimbievsky from the 175th Ground Attack Air Regiment was one of the most successful and best pilots in the 305th Ground Attack Air Division.

Hero of the Soviet Union and Yugoslav National Hero Major General A.N. Vitruk, who had only been head of the 10th Guards Ground Attack Air Division for a relatively short time, saw action over Hungary. In the autumn of 1944, he headed a group consisting of two divisions which played a significant role in the liberation of Belgrade.

Soviet aircraft in low-altitude attack on the Kecskemét railway station in south-west of Hungary.

A map of the Battle of Debrecen, which was fought by Soviet forces of the 2nd Ukrainian Front from 6–28 October 1944, with the aim of routing the German Army Group South.

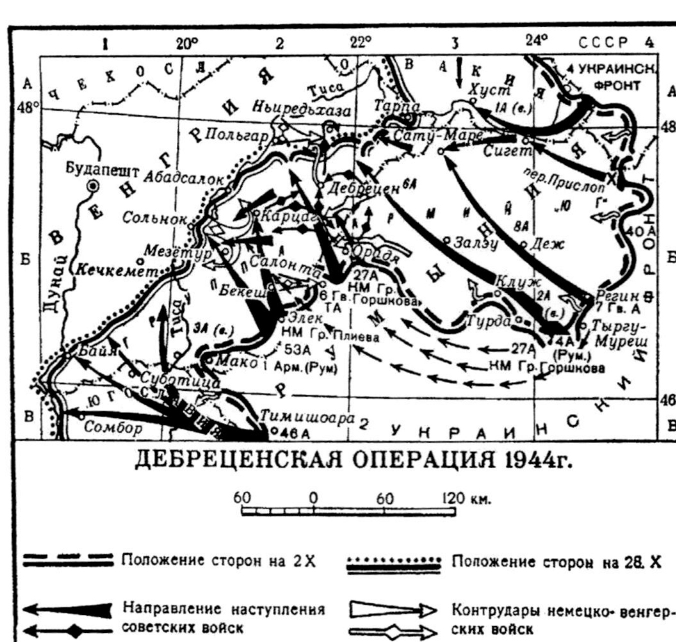

Hungarian fighter-pilot Leutnant Laszlo Mathe from 101/1 preparing for a combat sortie in the cockpit of his Messerschmitt. By the spring of 1945, he had recorded nine aircraft shot down.

Technical personnel carry out repairs to the M-62IR engine of a Soviet Li-2 night fighter in autumn 1944.

Li-2 transport plane of the 5th Air Corps being loaded with military cargoes (note the ammunition boxes in the foreground) in the vicinity of the Romanian-Hungarian border, September 1944.

Soviet and Romanian officers, in front of Lockheed Electra aircraft, discussing the further plans on the use of air force against German-Hungarian aviation, end of August 1944.

The same as on the left. Note Nicolae Ceaușescu on the left (in civil suit), the future leader of the Communist Party of Romania.

Technical personnel grouped together next to a Yak-9 from the 513th Fighter Air Regiment, 331st Fighter Air Division. The division formed part of the Soviet V Ground Attack Air Corps, providing cover for Il-2 aircraft.

A multi-role Me 210 with Hungarian Air Force markings comes in to land.

Hungarian Ju 86 and Me 210 aircraft captured by Red Army forces on Szolnok airfield. As a rule they were in a dismantled state.

This aircraft from the 951st Ground Attack Air Regiment (10thGround Attack Air Corps) was seriously damaged by shrapnel from an anti-aircraft shell. Also visible are the bullet holes in the aft section of the fuselage.

One of the attack regiment crews near Il-2 aircraft, 5th Air Army.

Soviet mechanics under the regiment's senior engineer repair the engines on a Boston bomber in autumn 1944.

One of the Bf 109G-6 fighters manufactured in Hungary under a German licence is prepared for a sortie.

Soviet motorized column crossing Tisza river. Noe anti-aircraft machine gun on the left.

The highest-scoring German ace Erich Hartmann and the Hungarian Laszlo Pottyondy standing by the nose of a Bf 109G-6.

Cows graze on an airfield. In the background is an Me 210 ZO + 99.

Hungarian pilots from the 102/1 in Munkacs stand near refueling tankers in September 1944.

Commander of the 17th Air Army, Colonel General V.A. Sudets arrived to one of the front-line airfields in autumn 1944.

Li-2 transport aircraft, preparing for a long-range flight from Bucharest to the area around Budapest, are loaded from GAZ-MM trucks.

Young pilot Yuriy Yablokov from the 1st Long-Range Air Regiment standing next to his Po-2.

German tank column entering Budapest, October 1944.

King's Palace in Budapest, before beginning of the combats for the city.

German tank crew and Tiger II setting up a position at the barricade for the coming battle in Budapest, October 1944.

The graduates of the Royal Hungarian Military Academy Ludovika (Magyar Királyi Honvéd Ludovika Akadémi) take their oath.

Soviet soldiers and locals pay their respects in memory of those who fell in the liberation of Debrecen.

Hungarian tank crews being trained by Germans on the Tiger heavy tank, October 1944.

Admiral Horthy (in the black greatcoat) takes a parade of the Hungarian troops.

Panther of German tank column is passing through the center of Debrecen, October 1944.

Loading an Si-47 transport aircraft with cargo intended for the forces of the 2nd Ukrainian Front.

German motorized column passing along outskirts of Budapest, end of October 1944.

German SS units in Budapest. *Wirbelwind* anti-aircraft vehicle is in the foreground.

3

Budapest: Offensive Objective

With the onset of winter, battles for the Hungarian capital unfolded with new intensity. Several major offensive operations by the Red Army (the Petsamo-Kirkenes, Baltic and Belgrade offensives) had finished, and active military operations along the Soviet–German front were conducted only in East Prussia and Hungary. Consequently, the *Luftwaffe* had an opportunity to reinforce their groups in these sectors: the number of combat aircraft in the 4th Air Fleet reached 721, the highest number for the whole of 1944. Furthermore, the German command strove to intensify aerial combat operations to the maximum possible extent.

On 1 December, the commander of the Soviet III Guards Attack Corps, General V.V. Stepichev, signed an order to conduct operations in support of the 7th Guards Army, 46th Combined-Arms Army and 6th Guards Tank Army. Stepichev outlined the area of contact with the enemy and the location of the German and Hungarian aerodromes and zones of intense anti-aircraft fire. He also ordered the delivery of a saturation strike on the enemy's artillery and mortar batteries on 3 December from 10:15 a.m. to 12:15 p.m., and the providing of immediate support for Soviet tank formations as they attempted to break through enemy lines. Groups of eight to 10 Il-2s were to remain airborne above the battlefield for at least 15 minutes, with the change-over of units performed in the air, attacks carried out from a 'circle' formation and repeat sorties made an hour and 20 minutes after landing. Stepichev added that the first day of the offensive should include 250 combat sorties.

However, the offensive started two days later than the planned date. After a week's redeployment, on 5 December the troops of the 2nd Ukrainian Front approached the Danube north and north-west of Budapest, thereby cutting off the enemy's withdrawal route to the north. The Soviet 46th Army performed a rapid crossing of the Danube to the south of the capital from the side of the Csepel Island, and successfully captured a small foothold on the far side of the river. General I.A. Pliyev, whose Cavalry Mechanized Group took part in the offensive, recalled in respect of the events on 5 December:

> We failed to breach the enemy's defensive lines through the entire depth, and the attack began to wane, so the Front Commander committed the 6th Guards Tank Army, which had to complete the breakthrough battle ... The commitment of the tank formation created a turning-point. The momentum of the offensive increased; it was further augmented by powerful strikes of our aircraft which flew in waves above our heads in the direction of the enemy. The roar of the battles moved away to the north.

Documents of the 151st Guards Fighter Regiment (of the III Guards Fighter Corps) recognize that in the second half of November 1944, the enemy's air force around Budapest became considerably more active and delivered several saturated strikes on attacking Soviet troops. The regiment, which took part in the battles with 30 Yakovlev aircraft at its disposal, including two brand-new Yak-3s, later observed:

> By the beginning of December 1944, the enemy had suffered aircraft losses, had lost Romanian oil supplies, and in conditions of huge damage being inflicted by saturated raids of our allies' air forces, was striving to retain its air force for the Reich's defense and thus reduced its activity in other directions. Our Air Forces commanded the air. Forward of the 4th Ukrainian Front, there were up to 450 aircraft of the 4th Air Fleet (among them 165 fighters, 155 bombers and ground-attack aircraft, 80 long-range and short-range reconnaissance aircraft and a group of miscellaneous communication, transport, and courier aircraft). The enemy's fighters tended to adhere to defensive tactics.

During this time, the 151st Guards Fighter Regiment lost its commander, as the regiment's report continued:

> On 5 December 1944, four Yak-1s and Yak-3s, with Regiment Commander Major E.M. Ravikovich as the lead, were covering our troops crossing the Danube to the south of Budapest; they were patrolling at an altitude of 1,500–2,000m. The group encountered two groups of approximately 20 Junkers Ju 87s and up to 20 Focke-Wulf 190s together with four Messerschmitt Bf 109s which were strafing our troops. Our aircraft immediately attacked to prevent pinpoint bombing. Major Ravikovich attacked a Junkers with fire from the upper rear and brought it down; the Junkers fell to the

north-east of Ersci. Major Ravikovich continued the air battle and was attacking the enemy's second aircraft when he was probably shot down from behind by an air gunner; [his] Yakovlev aircraft fell into a spin during the breakaway; the pilot made no attempts to pull the aircraft out of the spin. Other pilots of the group were engaged; there was no possibility to check the circumstances of the Regiment Commander's death.

Ravikovich, who had been flying the Yak-3 S/N 1519, was the only one of the regiment's pilots killed that month in 109 combat sorties. Two more Yakovlev aircraft were hit, but their pilots bailed out. From 6 December, the regiment came under the command of one of the most high-scoring Soviet fighter aces of the war, Major Sh.N. Kiriya, who had shortly before been awarded the title of Hero of the Soviet Union. German documents testify to the fact that on 5 December the Soviet regiment encountered aircraft from the *II/SG2*, with their only loss being a Henschel Hs 123, possibly shot down by anti-aircraft fire. Four obsolete Hs 123 biplanes had shortly before been handed over to the unit after repair. The German pilot who got behind Ravikovich's Yak-3 and shot it down was probably *Leutnant* H. Ewald of the *II/JG52*, who thus scored his 46th victory.

Throughout 5 December, crews of the Soviet 5th Air Army flew 803 combat sorties (with losses totaling 13 aircraft) to support their attacking troops, while the Axis air forces responded with 350 flyovers. *Luftwaffe* elements, in groups of 12 to 18 aircraft, bombed the attacking 7th Guards Army and 46th Army. In the sector of the neighboring 3rd Ukrainian Front, the intensity of combat sorties was much lower. For the following few days, low clouds and snowy rain prevented serious active combat operations by either side. "During 4 and 5 December, our regiment made 22 combat sorties from Nadal aerodrome; however, from 6–8 December, the aircraft were grounded because of continuous rain; the visibility did not exceed 2km, the ground was soaked, and the fighters could hardly lift off from the airfield," recalled the commander of the Soviet 611th Fighter Regiment, Lieutenant Colonel N.F. Isayenko.

Nevertheless, even in such weather the most experienced pilots were willing to fly. On 11 December, a group of Soviet ground-attack aircraft of the 615th Attack Regiment (10thAttack Corps) led by Major G.Y. Petrovets strafed the aerodrome of Tapolcak (Tapolca, south-west of Budapest, on the northern bank of Lake Balaton). A group of Messerschmitts bearing ace-of-spades signs on their engines suddenly appeared, and after a swift attack, one of the Il-2s issued a plume of smoke and crashed to earth near the airfield. The remaining members of the Soviet group succeeded in mounting a defense and seeing off subsequent attacks. Radio operator gunner Sergeant I.M. Dorozhkin made his mark in the action against the enemy fighters; then, with his aircraft flying at treetop height, he suppressed two anti-aircraft installations on the edge of the aerodrome by firing at them with his Berezin turret machine gun.

The German fighters also flew other missions, along with covering their aerodromes. *Oberleutnant* H. Lipfert of the *II/JG52* recalled:

> Together with my wingman *Unteroffizier* Brandecker [we] were loitering for almost an hour above the front line, but saw nothing, and it was only on our way back that I saw a solitary aircraft above Lake Balaton at approximately 5,000m. We climbed in a spiral and recognized that it was a Petlyakov Pe-2, the Russian reconnaissance aircraft. It flew westward without haste. But the Russian crew must have been on the alert, because when I took up position in the rear and was ready to open fire the Pe-2 performed a turn and descent and attempted to break away at a high speed. My aircraft became decelerated during the climb, and the Russian was at first able to increase the distance between us. However soon we were flying behind him again. Neither turns nor other maneuvers could help him, and the efforts of the aft gunner were also in vain. The flares were whizzing past our cockpit, but I managed to approach quite close, pressed the trigger of the 30mm cannon, and made two hits. Just one hit would have been enough; the other made the aircraft explode."

According to Soviet documents, a Petlyakov Pe-2 piloted by Lieutenant V.R. Yolokhov of the 39th Separate Reconnaissance Regiment did not return from the sortie on 11 December. For many years, Yolokhov, his navigator Lieutenant Ukhvatov and radio operator gunner Tishchenko were deemed as missing as their Pe-2 could not be found. However, Hungarian searchers recently located the aircraft at the bottom of Lake Balaton. It turned out that the reconnaissance aircraft had exploded in mid-air, testimony to the efficiency of the then-new German heavy 30mm gun and confirmation of the accuracy of the German fighter ace's memory. The aircraft was raised from the bottom of the lake as it was impeding boat traffic, and the remains of the Soviet aviators were buried.

On the days following 11 December, the weather was changeable and pilots from both sides flew sorties, even risky ones, when the situation demanded. For instance, on 12 December, the *Luftwaffe* used small detachments against Soviet forces, one of the infrequent occasions when Junkers Ju 87s bombed troops from low altitudes in a straight flight. At the same time, the forward-based Gyemrõ aerodrome (30km south-east of Budapest) was attacked by 27 German bombers (it was reported that these were Ju 88s, bit it turned out that they were He 111s). Several groups of Soviet fighters took off to intercept the enemy, but on their way back to base they suffered several non-combat casualties. One Yak-9 crashed and its pilot, Captain M.S. Mazan of the 85th Guards Fighter Regiment (6th Guards Fighter Division), who had scored 20 solo and three group victories, was killed.

Following evaluation of the situation in Hungary, the *Stavka* set new tasks for forces of the 2nd and 3rd Ukrainian Fronts on 12 Dedcember. The advance was to be further developed in order to defeat Axis forces defending Budapest and capture the Hungarian capital. Forces of General Tolbukhin's 3rd Ukrainian Front were ordered to make the main attack from the Lake Velence area in the direction of Bicske, advance along the southern bank of the Danube and cut off the defenders' westward withdrawal routes. Part of Tolbukhin's forces were to attack Budapest and capture it in cooperation with the left wing of the 2nd Ukrainian Front. To ensure better control of the two fronts' forces during the offensive, and to accomplish the intended objectives, Supreme Commander-in-Chief Stalin, in his directive of 12 December, transferred the 46th Army of Lieutenant General I.T. Shlemin, which had been fighting beyond the Danube, from the 2nd Ukrainian Front to the 3rd Ukrainian Front.

The subsequent clashes were extremely intense, with Soviet forces approaching Budapest from all sides. Colonel S.N. Grechko, Head of the Operations Staff of the 5th Air Army, later wrote:

> It seemed that we had to bring some more pressure on them, and the circle would be closed; however, the enemy was opposing violently. The enemy forces were still holding important communications [routes] and kept receiving replacements and logistic support as necessary for defense from the rear. Our Air Army was charged with the task to use our best efforts to make the most important communications unserviceable; furthermore, we were ordered to accomplish the task as soon as possible.

The Il-2s continued to provide the principal strike power of the Soviet Air Force. Sometimes the major role in support of the land troops was played by the forces of the 5th Air Army, while on other days this role was passed to the 17th Air Army. The opposing sides each reported claims of huge losses for their enemy, both on the ground and in air battles. Soviet reports focused on *Luftwaffe* losses resulting from strike attacks and defensive battles, whereas the Germans more often mentioned the Soviet losses caused by the success of their 'free-hunting' fighter aces. However, the successes of both sides in their respective reports were, as a rule, considerably exaggerated. Yet there were certain exceptions. For example, on 14 December, of seven Ilyushin aircraft of the 715th Attack Regiment launched in a sortie, five did not return. Among those reported missing were lead pilot Captain M.I. Nyukhalov, and Lieutenant V.V. Burlutsky, Junior Lieutenant Y.K. Berg, Junior Lieutenant Y.M. Timofeyev and Junior Lieutenant A.V. Shashkin, along with their radio operator gunners; Lieutenant L.N. Sokolov of the 116th Fighter Regiment, who had been in the covering party, was also shot down. German reports state that these Soviet losses were brought about by a Messerschmitt Bf 109 unit from the *I/JG53* wing, with two of the victories gained by *Leutnant* J. Worlitzsch.

A decisive assault by 2nd Ukrainian Front began at dawn on 20 December. The main assault force, which made for Esztergom with the intention of encircling Budapest from north, was supported by General N.P. Kamanin's V Attack Corps (under cover provided by Colonel A.P. Yudakov's 14th Guards Fighter Division) and Colonel N.K. Romanov's 218th Bomber Division (covered by Colonel I.A. Taranenko's 13th Guards Fighter Division). In the report on the actions of the attached attack unit, the commander of the 7th Guards Army, General M.S. Shumilov, observed:

> Units of the V Attack Corps, which were engaged to carry out preparatory bombardments for the breakthrough, delivered powerful bombing and striking attacks of the enemy forces that were on the defensive in the front line and in the nearest tactical depth, and inflicted heavy losses on them. The attack aircraft pressed the enemy to the ground by means of gun and cannon fire, and contributed, to a large extent, to the infantry's assault and, further on, to the complete penetration of the enemy's defense through the entire tactical depth.

One of the main factors in the operation's success was that the Red Army Air Force commanded the air over the battlefield. Despite adverse weather conditions on 20 December, the Soviet 5th Air Army made 429 sorties (with night-flying crews of the 218th Bomber Division and the 312th Night Bomber Division displaying the highest activity), including 80 sorties by the Romanian I Corps (two of whose crews did not return from their missions). In response, the *Luftwaffe* responded with only 20 flyovers. All this enabled the commander of the 6th Guards Tank Army, General A.G. Kravchenko, to successfully carry out his mission. A German counter-attack was defeated, and the troops of the 7th Guards Army, in spite of several attacks by groups of between 15 and 20 enemy aircraft, soon reached the Danube. Meanwhile, units of the 6th Guards Tank Army began to encircle the Budapest garrison. Throughout all these battles, the Soviet forces were supported by attack aircraft under the command of General O.V. Tolstikov. Those December days witnessed six or seven Soviet aircraft flyovers for each German aircraft that was seen. General Kravchenko later briefly summarized the actions of the 10thAttack Corps at that stage of the Budapest offensive: "All requests for aircraft support in battles for enemy facilities were implemented in an extremely accurate, timely and efficient manner.

Pilots of the Soviet 17th Air Army kept pace with their colleagues of the 5th Air Army, in spite of considerable losses on 20 December, when the 10thAttack Corps alone lost seven Il-2s and five pilots, two of whom were killed in crashes. Lieutenant V.S. Seregin of the 672nd Attack Regiment made his mark by breaking through dense German anti-attack fire towards his target and destroying two trucks and a refueling vehicle with his bombs. Breaking away from his strike, he noticed a Focke-Wulf attempting to shoot down one of his compatriots. Vladimir Seregin reacted swiftly, turning his aircraft, and firing a long burst to deter the Focke-Wulf pilot and thus most likely save the life of a fellow officer. After the war, Hero of the Soviet Union Seregin continued his service with the Red Army Air Force; from March 1967, the then Colonel Seregin was in command of a space pilot training regiment. He was killed along with Yuri Gagarin (the first man to reach outer space) when a MiG15-UTI training jet crashed in March 1968, and was buried near the Kremlin Wall in Moscow.

On 21 December, after launching 727 daytime mission sorties, pilots of General Sudets' 17th Air Army reported the destruction of large enemy forces on the ground (18 tanks were reported among the burnt-out vehicles) and in the air (22 downed aircraft), at the cost of 17 lost aircraft, including 12 Il-2s of the 10thAttack Corps. Again, the crews of the 672nd Attack Regiment distinguished themselves. Commander of the 306th Attack Division A.V. Ivanov, who was observing the group's operations from a forward command post, was especially impressed by the actions of radio operator gunner Sergeant A.P. Mikheyev. In an attack against a gathering of motor vehicles and troops near Bodajk, Mikheyev's Il-2 aircraft was itself attacked by a group of FW 190s; he repelled four attacks, and, when his gun seized up, he did not lose presence of mind, but promptly informed his pilot over the intercom and directed his actions to avoid the German aircraft's fire. Eventually, after a series of bursts of fire by the Germans, the stricken Ilyushin attack aircraft went down. However, immediately after touching down in a field, Mikheyev scrambled out of the cabin, extricated the wounded pilot, and carried him to safety.

The Soviet pilots rendered vital support to tank forces in the capture of Székesfehérvár aerodrome, where many German aircraft were leaving the base literally under Soviet tanks' fire. The Germans had not had enough time to mine the aerodrome or that at Börgönd. After an inspection of the airfields, Soviet commanders concluded that it was possible to arrange combat operations from there immediately after the redeployment of air units. The Red Army had by this time entered the Bicske area in the rear of the German defenders of Budapest, and kept on encircling the enemy. Using the aerodromes to support these land troops thus seemed an extremely attractive proposal. However, there was a danger that the Germans might seize the moment to destroy Soviet aircraft and vehicles during the course of their redeployment, with no anti-aircraft defense yet in place. Furthermore, intelligence information was received that the redeployment ferries would not be a surprise for German radar crews. Colonel B.A. Smirnov, whose 288th Fighter Division was occupying the airfields, recalled:

> As soon as our first aircraft landed, the enemy fighters appeared in the air. The 'Messers' and the Focke-Wulfs were flying from Veszprém aerodrome, which was the largest air base of Hitler's forces in Hungarian territory. Over 150 aircraft of various types were based there. The Germans had worked out a plan for an attack on Székesfehérvár and Börgönd aerodromes, but the German command had apparently failed to take into account the possibility that [we] would provide strong air protection for those aircraft. The enemy had miscalculated ... On the approaches to the aerodromes, the 'Messers' and the Focke-Wulfs suffered a squall of attacks; none of them succeeded in breaking through to any aerodrome ... In the course of redeployment of the division, it was not only in the air that the situation was turbulent. Fierce ground battles were going on 3 kilometers from Székesfehérvár and Börgönd; both aerodromes were subjected to artillery attacks. At the end of the same day, our last aircraft were redeployed; the forward technical crews and the logistics team arrived at dusk. Everything was in strict accordance with the detailed schedule. In the morning we could start combat operations in full force.

With the noose closing around the Hungarian capital, the commander of Army Group South, Colonel General Friessner, suggested an urgent redeployment and partial withdrawal of Axis troops from the eastern bank of the Danube. However, the Chief of the General Staff of the Army, Colonel General H. Guderian, forbade any withdrawal and invoked Hitler's instructions. Friessner later recalled that Guderian told him: "Führer believes that the loss of Budapest at the time of the successful German offensive in the West [referring to the ultimately unsuccessful Ardennes offensive, which had then just started] would reduce the efficiency of such offensive by 50 per cent."

Hitler had no doubts that a sudden attack in the West in the Ardennes would shatter the anti-Axis coalition. The fall of Budapest under the circumstances would have been a massive blow, so Hitler ordered that the city be defended at all costs. In the Hungarian capital, there was little sign of the impending danger. Trams were still running, the shops were open, trade was lively and the city-folk were getting ready for Christmas. The population had no desire to turn the city into a battlefield. The Führer, though, had different ideas; indeed, Szálasi's government fully supported him in fighting to the last soldier.

Many *Luftwaffe* units could sense the changes that occurred as a result of Hitler's decision to defend Budapest. The chronicles of the German 4th Bomber Wing recorded:

> The aggravated situation, taking into account Hitler's obvious position, called for decisions on the part of the German administration to stop the enemy's advance in front of Vienna's gates whatever it takes. Therefore, retaining Budapest was the top priority task. All the available forces had to be mobilized again. The fuel as needed for air units was provided from the so-called 'Führer's reserve' at the order of General Field Marshal W. Keitel [chief of the *Oberkommando der Wehrmacht*, or *OKW*, the Armed Forces High Command].

The period 21–23 December was marked by extremely intense battles on the ground and in the air, with many German counterattacks. The skies were patrolled by large groups of Messerschmitt Bf 109s and Focke-Wulf FW 190s. On 21 December, the *II/JG51* secured the most German successes with six victories, whereas on the following day, five victories were credited to the *I/JG53*. One of the *II/JG51*'s fighter aces, *Oberleutnant* H. Taubenberger, led the way with two downed Il-2s plus a Yak-9; his total score for December was six victories. The *Luftwaffe*'s attack aces kept pace with their fighter fellows: On 22 December, three Il-2 ground-attack aircraft were shot down by the commander of the *8/SG10* unit, Knight's Cross recipient *Oberleutnant* M. Goetze.

Based on the result of combat operations on 22 December, General Sudets, commander of the 17th Air Army, issued a special order analysing the causes of recent heavy losses, which totaled seven Yakovlev aircraft of the 288th Fighter Division and eight Ilyushins from the 189th Attack Division. According to the Soviet situation report, losses from all causes were 12 Il-2s and five Yak-9s. Sudets reported that German fighters often engaged the ground-attack Yak aircraft with heavy fire. To avoid such a situation, the commander ordered: "Ground-attack aircraft should operate in groups of 12 to 18 aircraft, with an escort patrol of six to eight aircraft. Forces should not be scattered over various detected enemy tank groups; instead, 40 to 50 ground-attack aircraft should be directed [to a single target] for 15 to 20 minutes, in order to destroy such enemy group completely."

The following two days were no less intense. The Germans credited *Oberleutnant* H. Lipfert of the *II/JG52* and *Unteroffizier* R. Goebel of the *I/JG53* with four victories each. It is highly probable that it was Goebel who shot down, on 24 December, the aircraft of the 672nd Attack Regiment's Squadron commander, Hero of the Soviet Union Captain N.N. Dyakov, for whom the 234th sortie turned out to be his last one. That was an exceptionally high number of mission sorties for a ground-attack aircraft pilot, and in most cases Dyakov had flown as a group's lead pilot. Unlike Dyakov, his regimental comrade Lieutenant V.S. Seregin, whom we have already mentioned, managed to bail out from his burning aircraft and find his way safely to Soviet lines. On the following day, several more experienced Soviet pilots did not return from their sorties, among them Captain D.P. Pivoshenko of the 951st Attack Regiment.

Lieutenant Colonel A.D. Yakimenko,who was among the few Soviet pilots in Hungary to fly throughout the Second World War, also addressed the recent reverses for the Red Army Air Force. He had had his 'baptism of fire' in the battles of Khalkhyn Gol in 1939 and was awarded the title of Hero of the Soviet Union for courage displayed in these clashes with the Japanese. Shortly before the beginning of the battle for the Hungarian capital, he had been placed in command of the 150th Guards Fighter Regiment. During the debriefing after one mission sortie, Anton Yakimenko instructed his men:

> The fate of Budapest is being solved. The enemy is exasperated. They brought their best forces here and will fight to the last drop of their blood. The battles will be fierce, though now they are not easy either. Courage and valor should be combined with prudence and calculated risk. We may not make mistakes. A mistake or a misjudgment in a battle means death. The slogan 'For Our Motherland We Will Die' is out of time. It served its purpose when we had the task of holding out and standing up. Now the task is different, that is, to destroy the enemy. And our slogan should be different, that is, 'Advance Till You Win!' We should defeat the enemy and survive.

As we have seen, casualties among Soviet flight personnel had been high, with many experienced and well-trained airmen killed or wounded. Consequently, there was felt to be a need to enhance aviators' psychological stability and self-confidence, which were positive factors for success. Yakimenko thus wrote:

> I remember the year 1939, Khalkhyn Gol, and battles with the Japanese aces. We had considerable difficulties at first. But the matter was not only that the Japanese pilots were strong, but that we lacked proper preparation, especially psychological. We flew well and made excellent shots on the 'cone', which was essentially a towed air target, and were good in training air combats. But all that was true for peaceful conditions; we were not yet accustomed to real risk ... We had to break ourselves psychologically, and that turned out to be a difficult task. But then Y.V. Smushkevich came and brought a group of pilots who had the experience of battles in Spain and China, among them B.A. Smirnov [later a division commander with the Soviet 17th Air Arm], A.I. Gusev, S.P. Denisov, I.A. Lakeyev, G.P. Kravchenko, and others. They told us what the Japanese I-97 fighter was like, explained the tactics of the enemy pilots and permitted piloting at low altitudes ... And thus the psychological barrier collapsed.

The commander of the 611th Fighter Regiment (288th Fighter Division), Lieutenant Colonel N.F. Isayenko, was another to acknowledge the serious situation in the air and the higher casualties towards the end of 1944. He described his own observations, saying that "As soon as our fighters approached the target, they were attacked from the top and from the rear." Sometimes, he said, Soviet pilots were able to repel the attack, but often they and their aircraft perished. "It was also discouraging that Hitler's pilots somehow always managed to be the first to attack," Nikolai Isayenko added. Among the men killed had been some very experienced pilots, in particular Captain K.L. Chernogor, who, shortly before his death on December 25, had scored his seventh victory. Isayenko attributed the recent problems that had occurred for the Soviets to the Germans' extensive use of radar stations and the fact that new fighter aircraft types had been put into service with German air groups in Hungary.

The Germans had indeed replenished their air fleet (first of all, the fighter fleet) with more advanced aircraft types. For instance, after its replenishment the *I/JG53* had at its disposal 32 Messerschmitt aircraft (all of them operable), among them Bf 109G-10/U4s, G-14/U2s and G-14/U4s (Isayenko had incorrectly indicated the German aircraft types in his report) with an improved aft quadrant view and more advanced modifications of uprated engines. Many of the new aircraft were fitted with two heavy machine guns and 30mm cannons mounted in the 'vee' of the engine units; some, in addition, had two 30mm cannons in underwing pods. In spite of the low muzzle speed of the new MK 108 auto-cannons, the weapons had high reliability and an excellent, for their caliber, rate of fire; a fighter aircraft fitted with such cannons could (provided there was a marksman in the cockpit) be an extremely dangerous adversary for Soviet aircraft (especially for attack aircraft) at a distance of 200–250m.

Although the *Luftwaffe* also suffered heavy losses in the battles that developed around Budapest, the attrition ratio during the last month of the year was clearly not in favor of the Red Army Air Force. However, on 22 December at least seven Messerschmitts of the *II/JG52* were shot down or seriously damaged at the Budaörs aerodrome, while one of the highest-scoring aces of the *II/JG52*, Knight's Cross recipient H. Sturm (125 victories), collided with a motor vehicle at take-off and crashed at Csor aerodrome south-west of Székesfehérvár. On the following day, Senior Lieutenant P.N. Parovin of the 151st Guards Fighter Regiment (III Guards Air Corps) shot down, at low altitude, an anti-tank Henschel Hs 129 to gain his 14th victory. That was quite a rare occurrence for late 1944, as the losses of the *IV(Pz.)/SG9* were usually brought about by fire from the ground or by technical problems with the Hs 129 aircraft.

Shortly after midday on 23 December, German fighter aces *Oberleutnant* H. Taubenberger (13 victories) of the *II/JG51* and *Major* K. Rammelt, commander of the *II/JG51*, who had flown 450 mission sorties and scored 41 victories (three of them on 21 December) against Soviet and Allied air forces, were shot down and badly wounded. Rammelt bailed out from his burning aircraft near Esztergom and flew no more sorties during the rest of the war. According to Soviet data, these successes were the result of an attack by pilots of either the 177th Guards Fighter Regiment (with the two victories credited to Senior Lieutenant K.S. Maltsev), the 116th Fighter Regiment (Lieutenants P.M. Dolgaryov and A.N. Sidorovsky in Yakovlevs) or the 92nd Fighter Regiment (Lieutenant P.V. Bondarkov with Junior Lieutenant Y.I. Meged in Lavochkins).

Throughout the offensive, the main fighting forces of the Soviet 6th Guards Tank Army, with continuous support from groups of ground-attack aircraft, were advancing to the south along the Grone River and attacking the flank and rear of German units executing a counter-attack against the 7th Guards Army. Meanwhile, the 3rd Ukrainian Front was successfully advancing to the north. They captured rich trophies near Székesfehérvár, among them 3,200 POWs, 10 tanks, 85 heavy weapons, 10 armored personnel carriers, numerous other vehicles and equipment, 54 aircraft, 19 steam locomotives, 622 railroad cars (100 of them carrying ammunition) and seven storage depots.Meanwhile, on aerodromes south of Székesfehérvár, Soviet troops discovered 28 burnt or destroyed enemy aircraft, and up to 100 aircraft in repair were captured in hangars and at the Germans' repair base.

The captured aircraft aroused particular interest. According to the 3rd Ukrainian Front Staff Report, during the period from 21–24 December, 106 aircraft were destroyed and 154 captured; however, most were essentially 'utility aircraft', i.e. for courier, training and communication use, while the rest were in an unserviceable or torn-down condition. The Staff Commission of the 17th Air Army determined that all 54 recently captured Messerschmitt Bf 109Gs had only shortly before been manufactured at the Kōbánya plant in Budapest under the German–Hungarian cooperation program; all that needed to be done was to fuel them and hand them over to their respective air units, but the Germans had not had time to do so.

Meantime, the Soviet noose around Budapest closed. RedArmy aircraft kept flying sorties to support the advancing ground forces and attack the Axis defenders. Situation reports of the Red Army General Staff state that the 5th Air Army performed 565 combat sorties, while the 17th Air Army outdid them with 928 combat sorties. According to Soviet data, 29 German and Hungarian aircraft were shot down in air combat or by anti-aircraft fire. Figures in the documents of Sudets' 17th Air Army Headquarters recorded that 953 combat sorties were carried out (including 136 at night), adding: "The bombing and striking attacks resulted in [the] destruction of 24 tanks, up to 250 motor vehicles, 150 carriages and 30 railroad cars; [the] fire of 18 anti-aircraft and field batteries were suppressed, and hundreds of the enemy's soldiers and officers were dispersed and partially liquidated."

Axis aviators were not passive either. On the night of 24/25 December, the *I/KG4* unit assaulted Soviet transport communications and attacked a bridge across the Danube near Dunafjoldvar. At the same time, the *II/KG4* continued, after a short break, laying spherical floating mines in the navigating channel of the Danube. The chronicles of the Danube Military Flotilla for 25 December recorded: "From 21.15 to 21.55 [hours], six enemy aircraft bombed the Danube crossing near Dunapentele [also referred to as Pentele, currently Dunaújváros] using photoflash bombs. Up to 22 bombs were dropped; eight of them fell down near the location of the mobile headquarters of the Danube Military Flotilla. During the daytime on 25 December, river minesweepers of the Danube Flotilla continued contact and non-contact minesweeping in the Danube navigating channel."

The last days of the year were spent in intense battles. Thus, for example, on Christmas Day the forces of the 2nd Ukrainian Front kept engaging German *panzer* groups and repelling incessant counter-attacks supported by anti-aircraft and assault fire, whereas the 3rd Ukrainian Front was attempting to bypass Budapest to the south-east. The weather was better on 25 December, with clouds breaking and the sun coming out. After sealing the German–Hungarian forces around the capital and forcing their way inside its perimeter, Marshal Tolbukhin's 3rd Ukrainian Front commenced driving the enemy from the suburbs and areas nearer the city centre, capturing district after district.

Upon receipt of data describing the fortifying of major buildings in the Hungarian capital which the enemy had determined to defend to the last man, Stalin sent a directive to the commanders of the 2nd and 3rd Ukrainian Fronts: "In order to prevent the Germans from implementing the plan [of long-term possession of the city], to avoid heavy casualties in our troops and to expedite capitulation of the forces encircled in Budapest, the *Stavka* of the Supreme Commander-in-Chief [orders the use of] artillery of all calibers including the heaviest ones and to use also aircraft and engineer demolition parties."

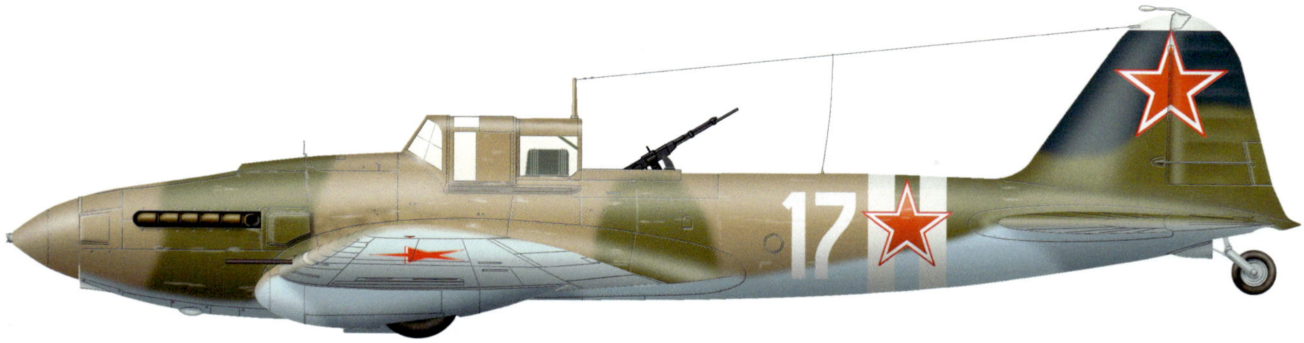

Il-2 of the 90th Guards ShAP, 4th Guards ShAD, 5th ShAK, 1944.

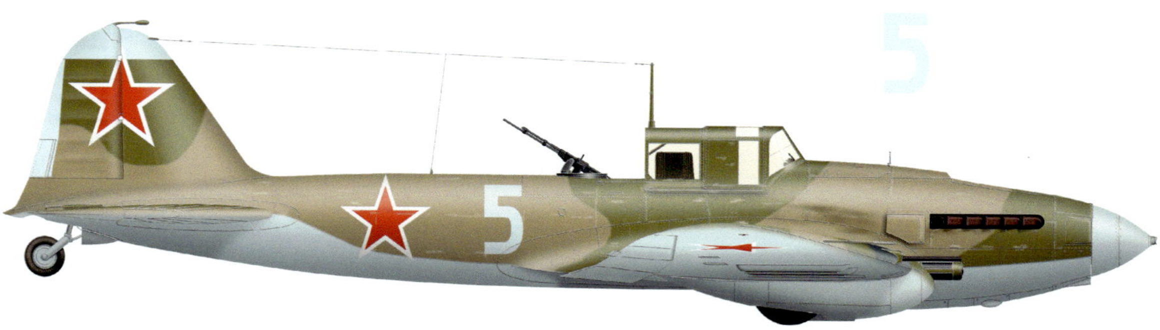

Il-2 of the 90th Guards ShAP, 4th Guards ShAD, winter 1944-45.

Il-2 of the 5th ShAK 1944.

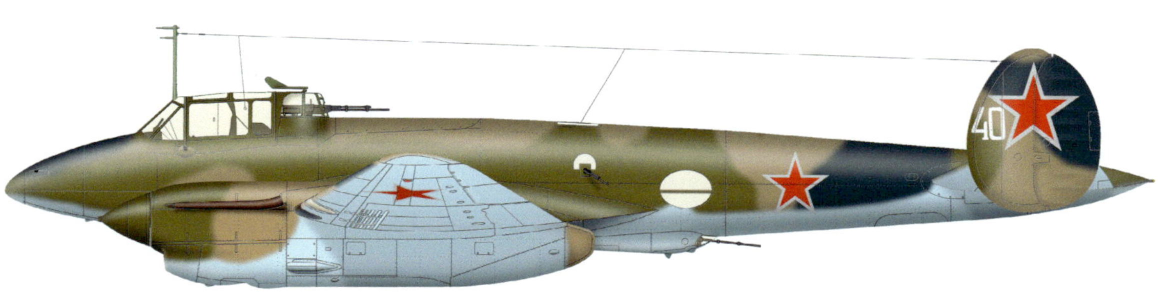

Pe-2 of the reconnaissance unit, Hungary 1944.

Yak-3 of the 31st Guards IAP flown by Lieutenant Colonel B.N. Eremin in the autumn of 1944.

Il-4 of one of the regiments of the III Guards Air Corps of the Long-Range Aviation.

La-5F of the 31st Guards IAP, 295th IAD, flown by Lieutenant Colonel G.F. Onufrienko, in 1944.

La-5F of the 164th IAP, 295th IAD, flown by N.M. Skomorokhov, late 1943 to spring 1944.

La-5FN of the 178th Guards IAP, flown by K.A. Yevstigneev, November 1944.

La-5FN of the 178th Guards IAP, flown by K.A. Yevstigneev, summer 1944.

Yak-9M of the 13th Guards IAD, Hungary, autumn 1944.

Yak-9M of the 13th Guards IAD, Hungary, autumn 1944.

A-20G-1-DO of the 27th Guards Air Regiment of night interceptors ('Blockers'), 4th Guards Long-Range Air Division, in 1944.

Bf109G-6 of the *101/I* unit, flown by *Leutnant* Laszlo Daniel, summer 1944.

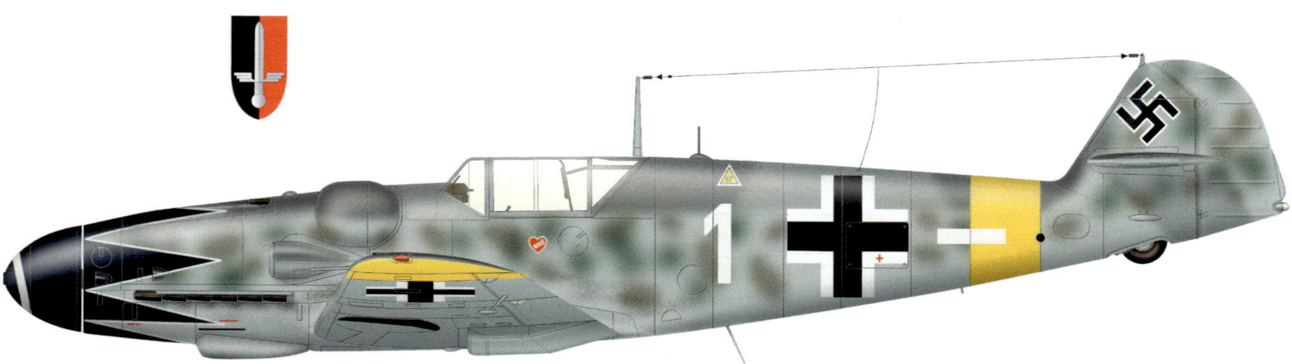

Bf109G-6 of the *4/JG52* unit, flown by Erich Hartmann, November 1944.

Fi 156C1 of the Hungarian Air Force.

Fw 190F-9 of the *II./SG2* unit, flown by *Major* Karl Kennel, Borgong, Hungary, December 1944.

Ju 88D of the *Wekusta 76*, Debrecen, Hungary, August 1944.

Ju 88D-2 of the 102nd Squadron, 1944.

Ju 87D-3 of the *102/2* unit, 1944.

Ju 87D-5 of the *III/SG2* unit, Slinka airfield, 1944.

Me 210Ca-1 of the *'Blyskawica'* unit, flown by Lorant Doczy, 1944.

Me 210Ca-1 of *1/102 Orzel* unit, 1944.

P-38J of the 82nd FG, late 1944.

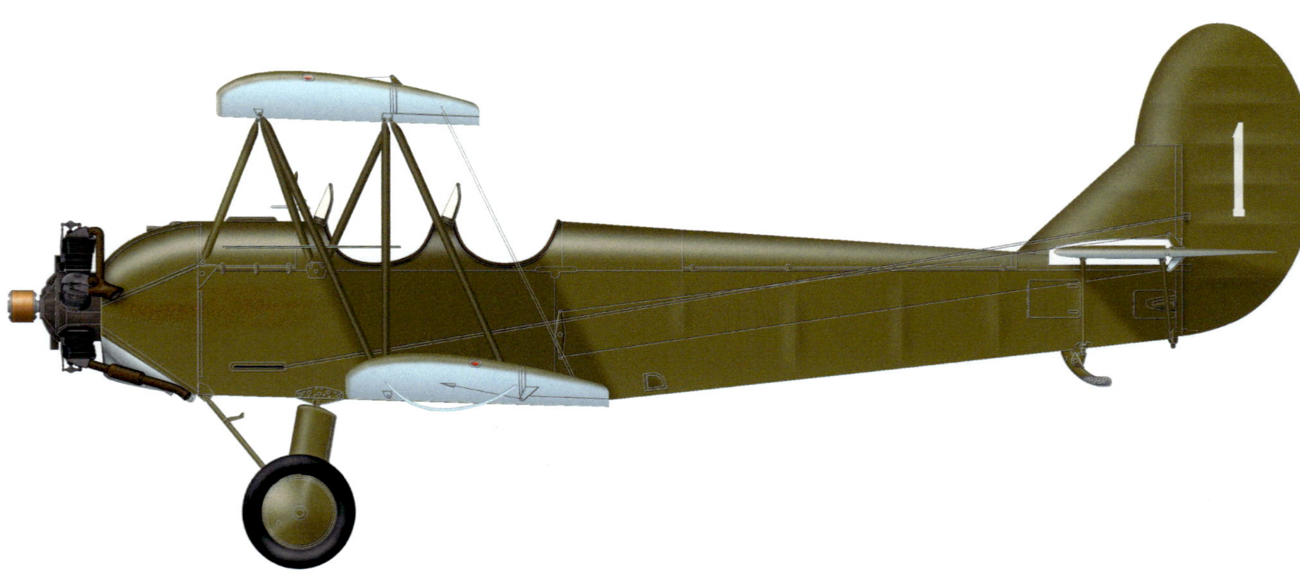

U-2 of the 1st Long-Range Air Regiment, flown by Y. Yablokov, 1944.

Hungarian regent Vice-Admiral Miklos Horthy, 1943-44.

Technician Nikolay Smirnov of the 151st Guards IAP standing near the tail of Yak-9 fighter.

The most famous and distinguished pilot of the Luftwaffe, H-U. Ruddel, who during the course of the battles for Hungary commanded the SG2 ground-attack Immelmann squadron.

Hungarian pilots receive correspondence on their home airfield on 11 November 1944.

The Hungarian Feldwebel Lajos Budai at the end of 1944. By the time of his death in combat on his 33rd sortie on 18 March 1945, he had recorded nine victories.

The commander of the Hungarian Fighter Regiment (101.V. Ez), Lieutenant Colonel Aladar de Heppes, opens the cockpit of a Bf 109G-6 following a combat sortie in 1944.

Mechanics align the undercarriage of a Yak-9 fighter belonging to the 149th Guards Fighter Air Regiment.

Soviet ace K.A. Estigneyev from the 178th Guards Fighter Air Regiment had attained 47 personal and three group victories by the beginning of the battle for Budapest.

This Yak-9 has stylized teeth on the cowling. The pilot is Junior Lieutenant A.F. Ivanov from the 85th Guards Fighter Air Regiment, who was killed in combat over the outskirts of Budapest.

Hungarian ace Molnar L. Debrody and his German colleague G. von Fassong (standing on the right wearing a fur hat) discuss the ins and outs of the previous air battle.

Pilot Molnar Lazlo is awarded the German Iron Cross 2nd Class in October 1944.

The commander of the I German Air Corps, General Paul Deichmann. In the course of the battles over Hungary, almost all the aviation units active in the region had been concentrated in his formation.

Deputy commander of the 6th Guards Fighter Air Division Lieutenant Colonel B.N. Yeremin standing next to a Yak-3 with the inscription 'From Ferapont Golovatov, the 2nd aircraft for the final routing of the enemy'.

Yak-9 fighters from the 13th Guards Fighter Air Division on a forward airfield in Hungary in autumn 1944.

German pilot E. Kuhlein from 4/JG51 and residents of Bulgarian village near Bf 109G-6/R3 fighter shortly before the unit relocation to Hungary.

Captain Evgeniy Polyakov, navigator, and later the Head of Communications of the 39th ORAP.

Crew of the 39th ORAP (17th Air Army) in front of their Pe-2 bomber.

Railway wagons bearing equipment and spare parts captured by Soviet soldiers in the outskirts of Budapest.

An FW 190F-8 ground-attack aircraft piloted by L. Varga from the 102nd Squadron, camouflaged on Borgond airfield.

A Bf 109G-14 with a ventral tank and its pilot Molnar Laszlo on Veszprem airfield in spring 1944.

Officers standing by the side of an La-5F belonging to the 177th Guards Fighter Air Regiment.

The German expert Gerhard Barkhorn (centre), who commanded the II/ JG52 group in the battle for Hungary, discusses the results of the latest sortie.

Hungarian and German pilots discuss the latest state of play in the aerial war at Veszprem airfield in November 1944. In the background is a Bf 109G-10 from 10/2 with an underslung tank.

An unknown Soviet pilot from the 5th Air Army in the cockpit of a Yak. The photograph dates from the end of 1944.

A-20 Boston bomber in Soviet service (presumably of one of the units of the 17th Air Army).

Crews (pilots and technicians) of a B-25 from the 13th Guards Roslavl Air Regiment following a special operations sortie in September 1944.

G.T. Beregovoy, who was the only pilot to be awarded the first Hero Star for the Great Patriotic War and was the second to make a flight into space. During the course of the battles for the liberation of Hungary, he led a squadron from the 90th Guards Ground Attack Air Regiment.

Pilots from the 31st Fighter Air Regiment standing next to a La-5FN that was manufactured from funds raised by collective farmers from Novomoskovsk. Seated at the back wearing his Gold Star is Lieutenant Colonel G.D. Onufrienko.

4

Intermediate Results for 1944

In their plans for the strategic offensive in Hungary, the *Stavka* of the Supreme Commander-in-Chief and the General Staff of the Red Army expected a decisive and significant advance. General S.M. Shtemenko, who at the time was Head of the Operations Department of the General Staff, gave an account of the arguments made by government and military officials for the continuation of the offensive:

> Taking possession of Budapest and force-crossing the Danube in a short time appeared quite realistic to us. The enemy infantry in the region was mostly represented by Hungarian divisions whose combat efficiency, according to our assumptions at the time, might have been radically destroyed by the anti-war sentiments that were building up among the population and by brutalities of the fascists who strived to keep Hungary in the wake of the Third Reich.

By the start of the offensive, forces of the 2nd Ukrainian Front had gained considerable advantage over the enemy in strength and means, especially in the main direction of attack. However, the Soviet Command failed to take into account the difficulties of fighting in a mountainous and wooded country and the over-fatigue of their troops. As a result, as early as October the Soviet forces were engaged in an intense military operation against a powerful enemy whose nucleus was composed of five German divisions and two Hungarian tank divisions. The Axis forces relied on a widespread system of well-prepared fortifications, and often committed standby forces, which were withdrawn from other areas, to action, while supporting ground troops with active aviation operations. Consequently, the defenders proved able to put up a violent resistance.

During the course of three months of hard battle, the forces of the 2nd Ukrainian Front achieved some success in western Hungary and captured huge amounts of prisoners and matériel. The 3rd Ukrainian Front of Marshal Tolbukhin, which was gradually put into action to render assistance to Marshal Malinovsky's 2nd Ukrainian Front, successfully forced a crossing of the Danube from 7–9 November (with support from the Danube Military Flotilla and aerial forces), then sedcured a large bridgehead on the right bank of the river. In mid-December, Soviet troops attacked the area around Lake Velence and Lake Balaton, leading to a breakthrough to the west of Budapest.

Within a matter of days, all three German–Hungarian defensive lines around the capital were penetrated, the Red Army captured the cities of Székesfehérvár and Bicske and engaged in combat in Buda, and the encirclement of enemy forces in Budapest around Christmas promised still further success. The German–Hungarian defenders, several thousand strong, under the command of *SS-Obergruppenführer* K. Pfeffer Wildenbruch, were now trapped in the city. The main political result of this period consisted in the forming of a provisional national Hungarian government in Debrecen, which terminated the nation's alliance with Nazi Germany and declared war on their former allies on 24 December.

Between October and December 1944, the 5th Air Army and 17th Air Army rendered considerable support to ground troops in breakthrough battles and pressing the advance, as well as in fighting enemy concentrations and standby forces. The Soviet air crews inflicted heavy losses on the *Luftwaffe* in terms of personnel and matériel. It was vital that both the strategic air domination, as gained in severe battles along the Soviet–German front in late 1943, and the operational supremacy in the directions of the main attacks in Hungary was retained by the Red Army Air Force. Consequently, Soviet ground troops were able to act freely and confidently, without much concern about their communications and rear areas, in contrast to operations carried out over the previous two or three years.

If we compare the results of combat operations of the Soviet Air Force in November and December, and take the 5th Air Army as an example, we may easily come to the conclusion that the efficiency of combat sorties increased in late 1944, while the role of ground-attack aircraft grew. All corps and division commanders, based at the command posts of combined-arms force commanders, were able to enhance the efficiency of attacks made by their subordinates, monitor the dynamics of battles closely and, day by day, keep improving interaction with ground troops day. Thus, for example, in the V Attack Corps, between a quarter and a third of all groups in the air were redirected to different facilities on account of a change in the ground situation at the time of the appearance of attack aircraft. In the III Guards Attack Corps, the air crews learned to conduct air battles in a more active manner, and more often forced the enemy fighters to break off and leave them alone.

Military operations in Hungary in the autumn and winter of 1944 showed that though victory was close, the struggle had not ended yet. The Germans and the Hungarian forces that were still resisting had not resigned their hopes of success, and many of their groups and units retained high combat efficiency. The Red Army Air Force Command demanded that commanders of aerial components should study their combat experience thoroughly, develop and implement in practice new tactical techniques, hold tactical conferences and meetings, constantly improve interaction between the air force and ground troops, and master in-flight aircraft control using radio aids and forward command posts. Among the many steps taken by the Red Army Air Force Staff at the time, noteworthy is the directive of 19 December 1944, which was addressed to commanders of air armies, air forces of military districts and commanders of air corps belonging to the *Stavka*'s reserves, and called for thorough study and implementation of new regulations and instructions.

Considerable attention was paid to the role and place of command personnel. Putting an end to frequent command changeovers was a positive factor. Consequently, of 28 air corps commanders within the RedArmy Air Force at the end of 1944, two had been occupying their posts for up to six months, six had been appointed for up to a year and the rest – including Generals V.V.Stepichev, N.P. Kamanin, I.D. Podgorny and O.V. Tolstikov – who were in command of the units fighting in Hungary had held their position for over a year. Young officers were boldly and energetically promoted to the posts of division commanders, while regimental commanders, according to the concept adopted by the superior command, were deemed key personnel in the Soviet Air Force (unfortunately, most of them seldom took part in combat sorties, in spite of their considerable flying experience).

Throughout the offensive in Hungary, the Soviet command replenished the air forces that were fighting there, as well as those operating in other regions, with aircraft of new types, such as the Yak-3, La-7 and Il-10. There were, though, certain peculiarities. Thus, for example, the 5th Air Army and 17th Air Army had neither Bell P-39 Airacobra fighter aircraft (which were widely used in 1944) nor the most popular Petlyakov Pe-2 bombers at their disposal (the latter were available only to reconnaissance units). On the other hand, both day bomber divisions, namely the 244th Bomber Division commanded by Colonel P.V. Nedosekin and the 218th Bomber Division of Colonel N.K. Romanov, were provided with Boston aircraft (primarily the A-20G modification), refitted with Soviet bombing armaments and some with small arms.

As for Soviet losses, many studies fail to provide an unbiased picture. For instance, historian S.M. Davtyan, summarizing the results of the 5th Air Army's military operations in December 1944, states that "in 8,245 combat sorties and 144 air battles, the pilots shot down 158 enemy aircraft; our army lost 24 aircraft". However, this account specifies only the Soviet aircraft which were brought down in air battles. If we take into account also those shot down by anti-aircraft fire, the aircraft that did not return from combat sorties and those destroyed during enemy raids on aerodromes, the total number of lost aircraft is 60. Furthermore, 26 aircraft were written off as 'non-combat losses'. In general, there was one combat loss per 137 combat sorties, which was quite a satisfactory figure for the end of the war. However, the Red Army Air Force Headquarters found the situation in the 218th Bomber Division unsatisfactory, with losses totaling nine A-20Gs and three B-IIIs, or one irretrievable loss every 30 combat sorties.

Perhaps for that reason, a tactical conference was held within the division in late 1944. The issues discussed at the conference included summarizing the results of operational use of Boston aircraft (those available in service included the A-20Cs, the already obsolete B-IIIs and the A-20Gs modified in the Soviet Union from ground-attack aircraft to bombers; the latter constituted an absolute majority), the use of Soviet-made small-arms and bombing armaments, and the operational experience with captured ammunition, including Romanian and Hungarian bombs. Issues regarding the further enhancement of operational efficiency of the Lend-Lease American aircraft were also discussed. Interesting data was provided in respect of command personnel of the 218th Bomber Division, as revealed in the table below.

The 218th Bomber Division joined the 2nd Ukrainian Front (5th Air Army) in April 1944, and before the end of the year made 1,649 combat sorties, including 365 nighttime

Rank and name	Position	Total flying hours	Total combat sorties/Total for 1944	Remark
Colonel N.K. Romanov	Division Commander	3,323	30/13	Flew all types of Soviet and lend-leased twin-engined aircraft
Colonel N.P. Rubbe	Deputy Division Commander	2,812	12/4	During 1942, trained and examined 47 air crews on B-25s and 53 air crews on A-20s
Major S.P. Osipov	Division Piloting Technique Inspector	225 for 1941–44	89/24	Had been occupying the post since 3 May 1944
Lieutenant Colonel V.P. Koliy	48th Bomber Regiment Commander	Over 900	69/18	Personally supervised the process of modifying the A-20Gs to fit Soviet standards
Major A.A. Panichkin	452nd Bomber Regiment Commander	120 for 1944	61/10	Flew U-2, UT-2, P-10, Su-2, UTI-4, I-16, ANT-40 (SB), and A-20 aircraft in all weather conditions, at day and nighttime
Lieutenant Colonel Y.P. Prokofyev	453rd Bomber Regiment Commander	110 for 1944	48/23	

ones. During the last days of December, in the course of raids against targets in the suburbs and in Budapest itself, some of the crews made up to two combat sorties per day, plus a sortie at night. Combat losses throughout the period totaled 38 aircraft (of those, 24 were shot down by anti-aircraft fire), while the Boston gunners brought down 19 enemy aircraft. During the period from April–December, the division's casualties totaled 26 pilots, 24 navigators, 41 radio operator gunners and 18 gunners (in addition to 20 flight personnel and four technical personnel being killed in crashes). A further 36 airmen were wounded, although most of them rejoined their comrades before the Budapest assault.

Meantime, captured Hungarian documents and evidence provided by POWs and line-crossers can lead us to certain conclusions regarding the state of the nation's air forces as of the end of 1944. In total, the Hungarian Air Force had approximately 100 combat aircraft (all of which were operated under the supervision of the German command), including 60 Bf 109s, 30 Me 210s and several FW189s; several hundred other aircraft were used as trainers or for other non-combat purposes. The *101 V.Ez.* air group of single-engine fighters, under the continuous command of Major A. Heppes, remained the strongest force, whereas twin-engine fighters were used for miscellaneous missions due to their high speed, powerful offensive and defensive armaments, and the availability of bomb racks and braking screens to perform diving attacks.

The Hungarian Air Force was under the command of Major General I. Banfalvy, who had before October 1944 occupied the post of Air Force Inspector General. Their main base was at Veszprém, which was where the training of a night fighter unit using the Bf 110G started. In spite of the serious damage caused to plants and aircraft repair shops by Allied aircraft raids in summer and autumn 1944 (especially to facilities in the cities of Szombathely and Győr and on the island of Csepel), the licensed manufacture of German aircraft continued; in early November, the first Bf 109G fitted with an engine that had take-off power of 2,000hp (higher than that of previous modifications) was accepted and handed over to the air units. The continued existence of a large number of experienced flight personnel who had joined the Hungarian Air Force before the beginning of the war with the Soviet Union remained a strong point of the Hungarian aviation.

The German General W. Schwabedissen, who had from October 1944 been appointed as chief of a special staff in Hungary, observed:

> At the time, night bombing attacks [by the Soviet Air Force] against tactical targets grew to a considerable extent; among the attacked facilities were transportation carriages, encampments, defense constructions, bridges and temporary crossings, aerodromes and headquarters. Thus, for example, the Russians attacked the headquarters of the temporary Army Group Heinrici in northern Hungary in mid-December 1944; in early 1945, they attacked the headquarters of the I Air Corps, and 'Hungary' support command headquarters in Veszprém, Pápa, Ődenburg [Sopron, to the west of Budapest, near the Austrian border] and Steinamanger (Szombathely). At the same time, the strike accuracy was low; therefore, results of the attack were minor.

It should be added that there were cases when the Soviet Air Force obtained good results in raids against forward positions, communications, and other important facilities just behind the German front lines. Generals of the *Luftwaffe* believed that the considerable increase in number of Soviet air regiments and divisions operating across the front lines, in combination with the reduction in number of German units (which, furthermore, from autumn 1944 had been experiencing frequent fuel shortages), brought about a situation diametrically opposite to that of 1941, when Germany's aviators were dominant during the opening stages of Operation *Barbarossa*. "On the other hand, the Russian, throughout the war, never managed to achieve ultimate supremacy," Schwabedissen continued. "That was due to the fact that, individually, Soviet fighter pilots were less strong than their German opponents. This impeded them from fully averting the attacks of German bombers and attack aircraft."

Many German pilots who could hardly be reckoned 'rookies' were confident that even during the last months of 1944, they had psychological superiority over their Soviet counterparts, and such confidence not infrequently helped them gain tactical victories. Thus, for example, *Unteroffizier* E. Rombach of the *II/JG52*, while far from being a fighter ace, was nevertheless well-trained, and fought successfully against English and American and later Soviet air forces. In December 1944 alone, he flew 36 combat sorties and shot down two Il-2s. Rombach pointed out:

> To become an aerial combat master, one has to have, along with piloting knowledge and skills, also good eyesight and quick response, and, furthermore, to be self-possessed and composed, to be able to size up the situation instantly. These are the qualities that an average Russian pilot lacks; what is more, they do not have enough combative instinct in an intense air battle."

According to German reports, the *Luftwaffe* did not feel much concern about the appearance of new Soviet aircraft types. The *II/JG52*'s commander, *Major* G. Barkhorn, was among the first to claim the killing of a Yak-3 in Hungary; upon return from a period of leave, he, according to a report of 26 October, shot down one of the new Yakovlev fighters. However, according, to Soviet documents, the German's victim was, in fact, an 'ordinary' Yak-9. Later, when the number of new Soviet aircraft types grew, and some of them were indeed shot down in combat, the Germans took almost no notice of them; their appearance, undoubtedly, did not have any demoralizing effect on the *Luftwaffe* personnel, including fighter pilots. Many Germans believed that although the Yak-3 had somewhat higher speed and better maneuverability at low and medium attitude than the Messerschmitt Bf 109G, the Messerschmitt still retained a number of advantages, including higher diving speed, higher lethality of weapons and better protection for the pilot.

There was another matter that was essentially of the greatest importance. A contemporary German report observed:

> As late as [the] end of 1944, the training and military skills of flight crews were still the weak point of the Soviet Air Force. As soon as the piloting skills [were] mastered and the air crews' morale and combat qualities rose (especially after the all-out assault by the Red Army), the combat capabilities improved; however, the Russians failed to correlate this with the ever-increasing numerical strength and constant modernization of aircraft. Therefore, the Soviet pilots, in general, were not very active in fighting. The situation assumed a critical scale in cases when the Russians had to face strong opposition on the part of the German forces.

With the primary task consisting in rendering support to ground troops and the air operations area deliberately confined to the front-line area, the Red Army Air Force only slightly distracted the *Luftwaffe* from completing their missions. Occasions when German aircraft were engaged immediately after take-off were quite rare. The table below provides an idea of German losses as per *Luftwaffe* documents; the number of German aircraft lost in air battles was relatively low:

The Soviet Air Force actively influenced the course of ground combat and performed a much greater number of combat sorties than their enemy did; however, nearly all air battles were fought in conditions of the *Luftwaffe*'s numerical supremacy. For example, during the days when flying was possible in November, the Soviet 5th Air Army's 1,149 aircraft had to fight against 2,930 aircraft of the German and Hungarian Air Forces, i.e. the force ratio for a typical air battle was 1:2.5. The Axis forces gained numerical supremacy by quickly concentrating their units and detachments above the critical battlefield areas. An evaluation of battles by the Headquarters of the 17th Air Army provides a similar ratio. This *Luftwaffe* supremacy was in spite of the fact that the command of the 5th Air Army created the special 'Sword' group of the most experienced pilots of the 150th Guards Fighter Regiment to build up forces in air battles. The group was equipped with the most advanced Yak-3 aircraft, and a considerable amount of preparatory work was carried out (in particular, reliable two-way radio communication was established between the fighters and ground posts, while the pilots were trained to obtain surprise in the first attack).

Indeed, tSoviet forces were unsuccessful in everything at the time; hence, the high losses of the Red Army Air Force in Hungary. In October, the losses totaled 125 aircraft in both armies; November added 132 aircraft to the count, and 199 more were lost in December. The German 4th Air Fleet, however, suffered the highest loses on the Soviet–German front; hence, there is the conclusion that the irretrievable loss ratio was almost 1:1, with 450 combat aircraft lost by each party. However, the Red Army Air Force flew at least twice as many combat sorties as their enemy, whereas the latter lost too many aircraft through no action of Soviet anti-aircraft assets; as discussed above, the Germans and Hungarians also failed to save quite a few aircraft when the Soviet troops were approaching Budapest.

Despite the encirclement of Budapest, the Hungarian capital still retained a large garrison to be overcome; final victory was still some way off, and the fierce battles on the ground and in the air continued. The coming of 1945 did not render the struggle any less intense. The following section of this volume chronicles the hard and bloody operations in Hungary during the next three months.

Month of 1944	**Losses of 4th Air Fleet**		**Overall losses of all Fleets in the East**	
	Combat losses	**Non-combat losses**	**Combat losses**	**Non-combat losses**
October	122	64	316	186
November	52	77	79	108
December	55	107	135	226
Total	229	248	530	520

The commander of the III Guards Fighter Air Corps, I.D. Podgorny. He began the war on the western Soviet border, commanding the 46th Fighter Air Regiment. He then commanded a division and formed a corps that earned the title of a guards corps. The III Guards Fighter Air Corps took part in the Debrecen, Budapest and Balaton operations over Hungary.

Helmut Lipfert's first combat sortie took place on 18 December 1942 near Stalingrad as part of the German JG52, and he attained his first victory on 30 January 1943. In total, up until 16 April 1945, he attained 203 victories.

The forces of the 2nd Ukrainian Front surged forward to storm Budapest in early December 1944.

Two of the Luftwaffe's most famous and decorated aces, Erich Hartmann (left) and Gerhard Barkhorn, who joined the "300 club".

A Yak-9 from an unknown unit of the 5th Air Army is readied for a scramble.

The 305th Ground Attack Air Division's airfield in the last days of the war.

Lieutenant Technician E.M. Agolakov from the 5th Air Army demonstrates to mechanics the idiosyncrasies of servicing an AM-38F engine on a ground-attack aircraft.

By the start of the battles for Hungary, Major N.M. Skomorokhov from the 31st Fighter Air Regiment had 15 personal and three shared kills in his tally.

A group of flight and ground crew of the 48th Bomber Air Regiment (5th Air Army) posing in front of the A-20G bomber.

A column of Studebaker trucks moving along pontoon bridge which was erected by the Soviet engineering forces across Danube river, November 1944.

Marines disembarking during assault to the south of Budapest.

Pilot Lieutenant E.K. Maskov stands on the wing of an Il-2 ground-attack aircraft following a sortie.

The fate of the commander of the III Guards Air Corps, General V.V. Stepichev, was similar to that of Podgorny. He started the war as commander of the 316th Reconnaissance Air Regiment, then led a ground-attack division and formed the II Ground Attack Air Corps, which became a guards corps and fought under enormous pressure. Between 1 June and 30 December 1944, units from this corps flew 12,027 combat sorties.

From 23 December 1944, General Balck commanded the Sixth German Army, which had gone into battle in the area around Budapest. At the same time, he also led Army Group Balck in Hungary (which consisted of the Sixth German Army and the First and Third Hungarian Armies).

The commander of the 150th Guards Ground Attack Air Regiment, Lieutenant Colonel A.D. Yakimenko (in the centre), with his comrades in arms on a front-line airfield in Hungary, with a Yak-3 in the background.

A Soviet ground-attack aircraft from the 10thGround Attack Corps on its home base, which had been damaged by anti-aircraft fire.

Left to right - technician V.I. Trezin, pilot Captain Z.G. Filkenshtein, navigator V.T. Tarazov of the 453rd BAP, 5th Air Army, standing in front of Boston bomber which was purchased on their own funds.

One of the leading aces of the 85th Guards Fighter Air Regiment, Captain Mikhail Mazan (left), talks to a colleague in a moment of calm.

Soviet officers posing on the frame of the shot-down Ju.87 dive bomber.

A discussion takes place in late 1944 at the headquarters of the 809th Ground Attack Air Regiment (V Ground Attack Air Corps) about a combat sortie. Second from right is the commander of the unit, Lieutenant Colonel V.S. Moskovkin.

The results of a raid by Soviet ground-attack aircraft on Hungarian and German forces in Budapest.

Personnel from one of the regiments of the 136th Ground Attack Air Division prepare for a combat sortie.

Armorers fitting bombs into the bomb bay of an 'Ilyushi'. Documents testify to the fact that Il-2s took off on sorties even from waterlogged airfields.

Soviet video operator arrived to the 6th Guards IAD for filming new Yak-9U fighters

Ju 87G-2 anti-tank aircraft on a long-range flight from Slovakia to Hungary to reinforce a detachment of the 10(Pz.)/SG2.

5

Battle on the Outer Encirclement Front

As is evident from German Supreme High Command documents, shortly after he received word of the encirclement of the Hungarian capital, *Führer* Adolf Hitler vowed to break through the corridor and rout the Soviet forces whatever happened, thereby enabling him to re-seize the initiative from the Red Army in the region. German General K. von Tippelskirch wrote in his chronicle *The History of the Second World War* (1951): "The liberation of the city and the area around Western Hungary became an obsession for Hitler, to which he subordinated any other thoughts, and which he would justify either by foreign policy concerns, or the urgent need to retain the remaining oil reserves in Hungary and Austria, without which ... it would be impossible to continue the war."

To raise the blockade of the Hungarian capital, the re-deployment began from just outside Warsaw of the IV SS Panzer Corps under *Ober-Gruppenfuhrer* G. Gille, as well as a single infantry division. The primary concern for the new commander of Army Group South, *General der Infanterie* O. Wöhler (replacing Colonel General G. Friessner, who had been dismissed) remained the fate of 'fortress Budapest' and the order for its liberation that came from the *Führer*'s headquarters. Before the arrival of the promised reinforcements, General H. Balck, who was now commander of the German Sixth and Hungarian Third Armies, was unable to count on achieving significant success with his worn-out troops. Nevertheless, Hitler required his commanders at all levels to lift the blockade of Budapest and restore the *status quo* on the '*Margereten* line' between Lake Balaton and Hatvan as soon as possible. The first transports carrying personnel and equipment from the reinforcement divisions entered Hungarian territory south-west of the city of Komarno on 30 December. However, it was to be several days before they could go into battle while the plan of attack was formulated.

Throughout the operational planning, designated *Konrad-1*, different ideas of how the breakthrough was to be achieved were discussed. The preference at the German headquarters was for the so-called 'northern variant'. This envisaged an advance from north-east of Komarno to the south-east, which, the German planners felt, had a good chance of achieving surprise. Moreover, thanks to the offensive that was unfolding along the shores of the Danube, and the powerful German LVII Panzer Corps that was concentrated on the northern bank of the river, the attacking forces' left flank would be covered. It was hoped that the offensive could thus be accomplished using a small number of forces and with minimal additional use of fuel in the redeployment of the mobilized units and could begin very early in 1945.

According to information from the Red Army Air Force headquarters, the crews of Pe-2 reconnaissance aircraft from the 511th Separate Reconnaissance Air Regiment revealed the formation of powerful German forces on the flank of General Kravchenko's 6th Guards Tank Army in good time. Owing to a lack of organization, however, no swift decisions were made to counter the threat.

The Soviet combined arms headquarters and commanders then admitted that the German counter-attack took them by surprise. The defense of the outer circle of the siege of Budapest was also deficient, particularly in the north, from where the attack was to come. To complete the element of surprise, the Germans launched the attack on the evening of 1 January without any artillery barrage.

At dawn on 2 January, the principal forces of the Soviet 17th Air Army took to the skies. Fighters provided cover for the ground troops, and patrolled predominantly above the city of Tata, south-east of Komarno. The largely cloudy weather was far from perfect for these flights. Nevertheless, General V.A. Sudets' aviators flew 671 mission sorties, while the enemy responded with 530 sorties, of which 455 involved the bombing or strafing of the 4th Guards Army's positions. The *Luftwaffe* increased the strength of their attacks day by day: there were 700 sorties on 3 January, then 900 the following day, which for the first time exceeded those flown by the 17th Air Army (773). This was an incredibly strong display by the *Luftwaffe* for this stage of the war. Furthermore, by no means were all flights made by German and Hungarian aircraft detected by Soviet Air Observation, Warning and Communication stations.

The *Luftwaffe* achieved notable success against Soviet tanks on 3 January, when groups of between 15 and 20 ground-attack aircraft circled almost the whole day above detachments of the XVIII Tank Corps, putting 16 tanks and self-propelled guns out of action. In the area around Bajna (north-west of Budapest and south-west of Esztergom), Junkers, Henschel and Focke-Wulf aircraft bombed and strafed Soviet armoured units, setting on fire six T-34s as well as 22 ISU-122s of the 110th Tank Brigade.

German documents reveal that the ground-attack aircraft that contributed the most to the success of such missions were the Hs 129B-3s, which were armed with high-velocity 75mm anti-tank cannons (a detachment of the *10(Pz)./SG9* at Papa aerodrome received five or six of these aircraft). These very slow and poorly maneuverable aircraft (two aircraft were shot down over the target on 3 January) were dubbed '*Buchsenoffner*', or 'can openers', by German pilots. Upon approaching the target, the pilot would usually be able to fire three or four shells, but one direct hit was sufficient to take out a tank or self-propelled gun, including the heavy IS-2s, ISU-122s and ISU-152s. The *Luftwaffe*'s fighter pilots were also to the fore; the German aces loved these weather conditions, which enabled them to make sudden attacks and then disappear once again into the clouds.

The Soviet 17th Air Army headquarters summed up the day's results in the report of the 306th Ground Attack Air Regiment (part of the 10thGround Attack Air Corps) for 3 January: "The Corps Commander has tasked us with: bombing and strafing the enemy after they launched a counterattack, and destroying personnel and equipment in the areas around Agostian, Tata, Bajót ... as a result of the Divisional Commander's [Colonel A.V. Ivanov of the 306th Attack Division] decision some 52 Il-2s were operational from 1010 hrs to 1700 hrs, flying 136 mission sorties." Since some of these aircraft were taken out of action on the first sortie, sustaining serious damage, the average load for a serviceable ground-attack aircraft was three to four sorties; some 28 Ils did not fly their sorties for various reasons, including Captain E.A. Seredkin's squadron (672nd Ground Attack Air Regiment).

In the course of aerial sorties, the 306th Attack Division's crews hit four tanks, 40 vehicles and seven carts (predominantly from the German 23rd Panzer Division), and eight seats of fire were identified. In a group battle, radio operator gunner Borodin shot down an Fw 190. Five Soviet crews failed to return after two battles with 12 enemy fighters, all of them from the 672nd Ground Attack Air Regiment: Junior Lieutenant Yakovlenko, radio operator gunner Sergeant Karimov, Junior Lieutenant Barsuk, engine specialist Yakimovskiy (who was flying in the gunner's position), Lieutenant Udalov, radio operator gunner Sergeant Mikheyev, Lieutenant Derbyshev, radio operator gunner Sergeant Shcherba, Lieutenant Kuznetsov and armorer Galitskiy. Some of the downed Ils were later discovered where they had made emergency landings in Soviet-held territory.

Thoughout the course of that day, the 17th Air Army flew 984 mission sorties (by day and night). As a result, 40 Axis tanks, 90 vehicles and seven field artillery guns were either damaged or destroyed, and three field batteries, as well as nine anti-aircraft artillery batteries, were taken out of action. Some 60 seats of fire were ignited, and up to 16 major explosions were observed. Around 480 enemy officers and men were scattered and many were killed. Four Il-2s, one Yak-9 and one La-5 were destroyed in aerial battles, while a further four Yak-9s and six La-5s failed to return, falling victim to German fighters and ground-attack aircraft. Soviet pilots claimed to have shot down 32 enemy aircraft.

One of the *Luftwaffe* pilots brought down and taken prisoner that day was *Leutnant* L. Duell of the *II/JG51*. Undoubtedly, many more German pilots would have been taken prisoner, as is evident from the diary of *Feldwebel* W. Opitz from the *I/JG53*:

> We had to fly over territory occupied by Soviet troops many times in the course of our free hunting. This was linked to us incurring heavy losses. Our commander *Major* J. Harder promised the pilots that anyone who had to make an emergency landing behind the front line close to Budapest would be evacuated using Fiesler Storch aircraft, capable of landing and taking off from short runways. As far as the author is aware, we used this method twice to return pilots back to their own lines."

According to German sources, their fighters flew 220 sorties on 4 January alone, shooting down 37 Soviet aircraft. *Luftwaffe* documents specifically underline the successes of the *II/JG52*, which claimed nine victories for the loss of just one Messerschmitt, which was written off following an unsuccessful emergency landing due to technical problems at Bábolnapusta (Bábolna, east of the city of Győr). *Hauptmann* G. Lipfert and *Major* G. Barkhorn claimed four successes each, each of their final victories of that day being the most memorable for them. Lipfert recalled how he drew up close to a damaged La-5 to destroy it, watching as the cockpit of the Russian aircraft simply filled with blood – his machine-gun fire had hit the pilot. For Barkhorn, the unit's commander, the success was noteworthy in that it became his 300th victory; the "expert", to use a figure of speech coined by authors R. Toliver and T. Konstebl, followed *Major* E. Hartmann (who achieved 352 victories against Barkhorn's eventual 301) into the *Luftwaffe*'s '300 club', which only had two members.

In light of the significant mobilization of German aviation, the Soviet command rapidly maneuvered their anti-aircraft weapons. Despite the small number of and heavy wear on vehicles in the 9th Anti-Aircraft Artillery Division, Colonel N.A. Roshchitskiy succeeded in swiftly transferring two reigments of small-caliber guns to defend the troops at Komarno, on the 46th Army's outer front line (they were also covered by anti-aircraft units from the II[d] and IV Mechanized Corps). More than half of the troops and equipment that the division had at its disposal (out of the formation's total of 16 captured 88mm guns, 81 Soviet-made 37mm guns and 58 anti-aircraft machine guns) took up their positions, the self-propelled anti-aircraft artillery having to simultaneously do battle with *panzers* as well as German aircraft (the small-caliber anti-aircraft artillery also employed against lightly armored vehicles).

Soviet anti-aircraft artillery crews became the main target for any FW 190s that suddenly appeared, and inflicted losses on the German raiders. One of the FW 190Fs aircraft shot down on 4 January was flown by Cavalier of the Knight's Cross recipient *Kapitän* M. Goetze, who had flown around 800 mission sorties. According to German records, Goetze had recorded kills of 32 tanks, 12 anti-aircraft batteries and 12

BM-13 'Katyusha' mobile rocket launchers in his tally. From the end of 1943, he not only attacked ground targets, but also skillfully engaged Soviet aircraft in combat. On the day that Goetze was killed he had already shot down two Il-2s, and his final tally was 16 when he was killed close to Pápa when his Focke-Wulf was hit by an anti-aircraft shell.

It is interesting to note that in the first four days of 1945, some 125 Soviet Po-2 aircraft belonging to the 262nd Night Bomber Air Division or the 14th Heavy Reconnaissance Air Regiment redeployed 137.5 tons of bombs, 293 tons of ammunition and 53 tons of aviation fuel across the Danube, a total of 483.5 tons of various cargoes moved in 1,095 sorties. It is clear that the 'crop-sprayer' Po-2s could not compete with the capabilities of the German Junkers transport aircraft, but this disadvantage was balanced by their ability to fly up to 15 sorties a day. Notwithstanding this, the Soviet command understood the need to provide more active assistance to the forward units of the 3rd Ukrainian Front, and specifically to the 17th Air Army, given the small number of Danube crossing points and their unreliability.

Soviet operations reports reveal that encounter battles continued over the course of 6 January, with the 46th Army of the 3rd Ukrainian Front beating back attacks from the SS Division *Totenkopf*, which were undertaken along the southern bank of the Danube and the road from Komarno to Budapest. While the 46th Army relinquished the city of Esztergom, it dug in to the east. The Germans were then attacked in their flank by the Soviet 6th Tank Army. Despite the significant cloud cover, fog and smoke over the battlefield, aviation played an active role: units from the *Luftwaffe*'s I Air Corps flew around 400 sorties, including up to 50 to transport supplies into Budapest, while detachments of between five and 15 ground-attack aircraft attacked Soviet troop concentrations. Crews of the Soviet 5th Air Army claimed 19 victories in 401 sorties, while the 17th Air Army recorded nine aircraft destroyed over the course of 670 sorties; anti-aircraft crews of the 3rd Ukrainian Front also claimed two aircraft shot down.

According to German chronicles, losses among their combat aircraft were not 30 (as the Soviets claimed), but just three or four, predominantly Bf 109s. They lost a further five or six transport aircraft to anti-aircraft artillery, as well as due to gunfire at landing places in the capital. The Germans claimed 13 Soviet aircraft were shot down.

On this day, the Soviet 5th Air Army flew 180 sorties to support neighboring formations and in defense of the outer front. The Soviet Command attempted to halt the advancing SS divisions with a massive attack by the 244th Bomber Air Division, with cover from the 295th Fighter Air Division, along the enemy's forward line east of Esztergom. This undoubtedly had an effect on the tempo of the German operation, with cannon and rocket artillery used to see off the Soviet attack. During this time, a group of Bostons took the commander of the 17th Air Army himself, General Sudets, into battle with them!

The commander of the V Ground Attack Air Corps, General N.P. Kamanin, kept a diary of the action along the front line, despite a ban on so doing. On 6 January he observed:

> On 3 and 4 January the Germans continued to advance east of Esztergom in the direction of Budapest. Some 25km stood between them and the capital. This breakthrough was of great concern to the Front Line Commander Marshal Malinovsky. To balance the German successes in this direction the 7th Guards Combined Arms and the 6th Guards Tank Army are to go on the offensive north of Esztergom. They are to attack in a westerly direction with the aim of getting behind the attacking German lines. The decision on the attack was dictated by the situation, but the chances of success are not good, [as] our troops in our armies have been depleted ...
>
> The air forces have no more than 30 percent of the standard compliment of aircraft at their disposal. They have to comfort themselves in the fact that the enemy does not have any large reserves of forces with which to fight us. There are only 93 ground-attack aircraft and 67 fighters in the Corps. The V Ground Attack Corps has not received any reinforcements in terms of pilots, or aircraft for more than six months ... The forces that are surrounded have assembled a striking force in Buda and are trying to break through to encounter the advancing German forces from Esztergom. The threat of a breakthrough in the siege of Budapest has been created. The Commander of the Ground Army asked me to provide urgent air cover.

By 6 January, thanks to the measures that the Soviet Command had undertaken with an urgent redeployment of the forces threatened with encirclement, Operation *Konrad-1* came to a halt. However, the Germans swiftly made another attempt at a breakthrough, which was known as *Konrad-2*. Many German generals were optimistic, as by the start of the offensive, more units forming part of the IV SS Panzer Corps had arrived. Although the SS formation could now advance with its full complement, the forces had incurred significant losses in the first week of 1945. The commanders of Army Group South then decided to expand the attacking front by incorporating into it the III Panzer Corps (known as the 'Breith' group). By 9 January, it became clear that *Konrad-2* had also failed.

"On that day the VII Mechanized Corps attacked with the aim of removing the threat of an encirclement of the Soviet defense by advancing German units," wrote the historian K. Ungvari. Over the course of 9 and 10 January, aircraft were all but inactive due to poor weather conditions, but this changed on the next day. In the course of difficult and ferocious fighting, 57 Soviet tanks from the VII Mechanized Corps (out of 80) were taken out of action and set ablaze. The Germans, however, lost around 100 tanks, thereby halting their advance towards Budapest. As Ungvari emphasized, the Russians "succeeded in retaining convenient strongholds from which they could attack in the future".

With the weather letting up slightly, General Sudets' 17th Air Army pilots flew 606 sorties, which helped ease the pressure on the ground forces. An order issued by the Military Council of the 4th Guards Army, whilst underlining the

Table depicting changes to Soviet 17th Air Army c. early 1945: Aircraft type, numbers of combat-ready aircraft and those under repair/maintenance				
	17th Air Army			
	Type	1 January	5 January	10 January
Fighters	La-5	79/15	76/43	213/17
	Yak-9, Yak-3	202/13	168/31	233/28
Ground-attack aircraft	Il-2	345/27	242/75	423/32
Bombers	A-20G, B-III	98/13	94/17	101/12
Night bombers	Po-2	94/3	94/3	103/1
Reconnaissance aircraft	Pe-2	12/2	10/3	15/8
	Yak-9	2/6	2/6	9/2
Spotter aircraft	Il-2	17/4	15/1	21/0
	Yak-9	12/0	8/4	12/0
Total		**861/73**	**709/183**	**1130/100**

cooperation across all the branches of the front-line forces, and the enormous part played by the aviators in beating back the enemy's push, stated in an address to the 17th Air Army: "On 11 January 1945 in fierce battles in the area around Zamol with a powerful enemy tank alignment, pilots under Major General Belitsky [189th Ground Attack Air Regiment], Lieutenant General Tolstikov [10thGround Attack Air Corps] and Hero of the Soviet Union Colonel Smirnov [288th Fighter Air Division], after attacking the enemy's mechanized forces with deadly fire from their aircraft, which had the greatest possible impact on the entire course of the battle, along with the glorious artillerymen and infantry, halted the enemy's plans to break through to the east in a *blitzkrieg* attack."

The Germans counter-attacked again with Operation *Konrad-3*, which was prepared in just two or three days. After regrouping and reinforcing their units, General Wöhler had, by the evening of 17 January, drawn together the entire IV SS Panzer Corps for the offensive, with some 644 tanks and assault guns, of which 526 were concentrated in the direction of the main attack near Lake Balaton. The expanse between this lake and Székesfehérvár was almost ideal for deploying tanks: a slightly hilly steppe plain with distinct forests and groves. The light snow cover did not prevent armored vehicles from maneuvering and enabled the Germans to bring their numerical advantage to bear. While the 3rd Ukrainian Front could field 377 tanks and self-propelled guns, in the spearhead the Germans created a four to 10-fold advantage in personnel and equipment. As far as aircraft were concerned, however, the upper hand remained with the Red Army Air Force.

On 7-8 January, the 17th Air Army received reinforcements in the shape of aircraft and crews. The Germans and Hungarians had at this time around 700 aircraft in the 4th Air Fleet under Colonel General O. Dessloch, taking into account transport command but not including Slovakian Air Command aircraft.

The Soviets were able to make good their losses with the introduction of the 194th Fighter Air Division under Colonel F.N. Dementyev, armed with La-5s. Moreover, the forces of this division were far from fully utilized: although the situation to the west and south-west of Budapest was complex and the *Luftwaffe* frequently held the numerical upper hand in air combat. For the most part, it was the division's 530th Fighter Air Regiment alone that fought in these battles, a unit which had at that time just 39 combat-capable crews, while the other two regiments – the 56th and the 848th – were only involved in ferrying matériel from Bulgaria (Yambol and Sofia) to the new posting in Hungary (at the Alibunar and Madocha aerodromes).

Soviet sources point out the enemy's numerical advantage in terms of combat aircraft in Hungary at the beginning of 1945, but this does not necessarily reflect how things were. The 4th Air Fleet of the *Luftwaffe*, as of 4 January (and there were no significant changes within the space of a few days in the middle of January), had been reduced because of the departure to eastern Germany of *SG2* (minus the I group). The fleet now had 588 German combat aircraft (78 single-engine fighters, 56 bombers, 199 ground-attack aircraft, 101 night ground-attack aircraft, 38 long-range reconnaissance aircraft, 67 short-range reconnaissance aircraft and 49 transport aircraft) They were, however, as well asthe 17th Air Army of the 3rd Ukrainian Front, also facing the 5th Air Army of the 2nd Ukrainian Front, giving the Soviets an overall almost three-fold advantage. Despite this, the correlation of forces for the *Luftwaffe* here was more favorable than for its elements then operating in Poland or Pomerania.

A report from the reconnaissance section of the 17th Air Army's headquarters mentions the significant successes of the aerial reconnaissance crews. The 10thGround Attack Corps flew almost half of all the reconnaissance sorties. The crews of the 39th Separate Reconnaissance Air Regiment photographed the main railway junctions and aerodromes in the middle of the month, and after compiling several photographic maps, the reconnaissance crews of the 454th Bomber Air Regiment photographed the Axis line of defense between Lakes Balaton and Veletse. Meanwhile, their colleagues from the 392nd Artillery Regiment controlled movements along the border roads and onwards to the front line by night. Notwithstanding this, the German regrouping from the Esztergom area to the northern edge of Balaton, which ceased on 17 January, was not discovered, which headquarters officers later put down to the poor weather conditions. Front-line reconnaissance was not at its best either. As a result, the Soviets were not prepared for the subsequent German attack of *Konrad-3*.

Just before dawn on 18 January, after a short artillery barrage, four German *panzer* divisions went on the offensive. True to their usual tactics, the Germans attacked several sectors at once, concentrating their forces on a narrow front and testing the defenses. A short time later, one of the German troop alignments set out for Székesfehérvár, while another aimed for the Danube, planning to reach the river at Dunapentele, in an attempt to divide Marshal Tolbukhin's front line in two. The situation for Soviet aviation units was complicated by the fact that they were based near the front line. The Military Council had received an order at the end of December 1944 that aircraft should be based as close as possible to the front line, since it seemed at the time like the constant advance westwards would continue.

The first night of *Konrad-3* turned out to be exceptionally stressful for the crews of the 288th Fighter Air Division under Colonel B.A. Smirnov. The 17th Air Army commander, General Sudets, recalled:

> The pilots of the 288th Fighter Air Division showed unprecedented courage that night. Their regiments were based on aerodromes in Székesfehérvár, Börgönd and Szeregeish (Szentendre) [all approximately 50–70km south-west of Budapest]. This lay in one of the principal directions of the enemy's third attack. In inclement weather conditions when the cloud base did not exceed 200–300m, the fighters along with the ground-attack aviation units routed an advancing enemy alignment. The front-line commander ordered that these aerodromes not be abandoned. In the afternoon of 18 January up to 130 German tanks broke through on the road from the west to Székesfehérvár. At the same time, Marshal F.I. Tolbukhin sent a rifle division forward from his reserves to take the defenses south-west of the city. Colonel B.A. Smirnov was ordered to hold the aerodromes until morning and carry out air attacks on enemy tank columns to prevent them from reaching Budapest.

At dawn, when the fog had dissipated and the visibility enabled air combat operations to begin, Soviet fighters took to the skies. What is more, they took off straight from their parking places, hardly warming up their engines. Several aircraft did drop bombs on the enemy, but the majority strafed the German troops, after which they departed for their forward operating aerodrome at Bregende, which was not under immediate threat of capture. However, German losses from air attacks were minimal. Meanwhile, General M.P. Stupin, the head of logistics of the 17th Air Army, located just outside Székesfehérvár, along with the chief engineer of the 288th Fighter Air Division, Engineer-Major N.I. Alimov, inspected all the equipment that had been left behind. Since they did not find any abandoned aircraft, they ordered the aerodrome's structures to be prepared for demolition and the runway to be mined.

The 262nd Night Bomber Air Division under General S.I. Tishchenko, located in the area around Perkat, which the German tanks reached on the first day of the offensive, was not in the best of shape. Despite the obvious threat of capture of its personnel and equipment by the enemy, the division's regiments did not abandon the aerodrome complex straight away, continuing to inflict night attacks on the Germans. Meanwhile the engineering and technical personnel, who were rapidly armed with rifles and grenades in response to an order from the commander, took up a defensive position on the edges of the aerodrome, rolling out their anti-aircraft guns to fire at ground targets. Night raids on the bridges across the canal at Szerviz (the small tonnage of bombs was balanced by high levels of accuracy), as well as on concentrations of motorized German infantry, proved to be quite successful; only on the morning of 20 January did Po-2 aircraft flee across the left bank of the Danube. The main cohort of technical personnel and logistics troops made their way along impassable and mud-swamped roads, under fire and subject to bomb attacks, to reach the site of their new deployment.

On the orders of III Guards Fighter Air Corps commander General I.D. Podgorny, the commander of the 14th Guards Fighter Air Division, A.P. Yudakov, in a Willys MB jeep, along with leading ace Captain K.A. Yevstigneyev and a radio set, mounted on the back of a Studebaker truck, set off on 18 January for the crossing point situated close to Dunaújváros. It was not easy to cross over to the right bank of the Danube north-east of Lake Balaton, from where they would be able to observe and direct Soviet aircraft movements. Yevstigneyev recalled:

> At the crossing point was a Babylonian stampede. The road up to the landing stage was packed to its limits with equipment: tanks, artillery, vehicles – all butting up against one another. It was not like you could get past, that was impossible! We tried to wriggle over the top – of the tanks, artillery pieces, tractors, vehicles ... This was an extraordinary concentration of military guns, set out in 20 rows that extended from the very beginning of the crossing point right out to the depths of the forest some 5 or 6 kilometers away ... After an air raid by Focke-Wulfs for me much of this scene would become unclear and strange. I could not understand what this was – an inability to organize things on the part of the command, or an overall disregard for an enemy that was growing weaker by the day? Such a gathering of the reserves of personnel and military hardware, and everything was all of a sudden bereft of air cover. A pair, or even a flight of fighters at the very least would have been necessary. What is more, there were several anti-aircraft artillery guns in this mass of hardware but the barrels were lowered down and had covers on. Only one small launch fired at the 'Fokkers' and did not stop even for a second. The same could not be said of the abruptness and cunning of the enemy.

Soviet aviation, however, was not passive at this stage. The main attack force remained the ground-attack aircraft, which operated at low altitude using anti-tank bombs and rockets. The commander of the 10thGround Attack Air Corps, General O.V. Tolstikov, had informed 17th Air Army headquarters more than once of his unit's actions and the difficult position that had unfolded in the 4th Guards Army's sector. The formation headquarters, as well as Marshal Tolbukhin's command post, was under threat of capture by the enemy. Urgent steps had to be taken. "At this difficult time the Supreme Commander I.V. Stalin, after speaking to the front-line commander, approved our decision to remain with our troops on the right bank of the Danube and provided assistance, sending us the XXX Rifle and XXIII Tank Corps," recalled front-line Military Council member Lieutenant Colonel A.S. Zheltov.

After evaluating the situation, 17th Air Army commander Sudets immediately sent his deputy in the Aviation and Engineering Service, Colonel Engineer A.L. Shepelev, to Madoche aerodrome on the right bank of the Danube, east of Balaton (a location that had previously been so hard to reach) to organize the evacuation of the remaining aircraft. Aleksey Lavrentyevich Shepelev recalled:

> On arrival at the crossing point at Dunafjoldvar I was greeted by a scene reminiscent of the dark days of 1941. Reserve units that had been tasked with blocking the route for the enemy that had broken through and restoring the *status quo*, were hurrying to cross the Danube from the left bank. On the right bank the approaches to the bridge were interspersed with vehicles carrying the wounded, as well as medical personnel from the hospitals; they were also carrying personnel and cumbersome equipment from the Army logistics forces. The enemy had already beaten us back from the other bridges across the Danube, [and] their tanks were some 8km from Dunafjoldvar. Given the stampede on the bridge, and on either side, it was hard to count on the implementation of any kind of discipline or order. What is more, the bridge was under constant enemy air attack; the severe air battles did not let up overhead.

The *Luftwaffe* succeeded in briefly recapturing the initiative. The troops of the 4th Guards Army suffered the most from air attacks, and there is an eloquent entry for 19 January in the army's combat journal concerning the actions of the *Luftwaffe*: "The weather was glorious, and in the skies enemy aviation held air superiority, since they did not encounter any resistance from our aircraft." Similar sentiments can be found in the combat journals of the 252nd Rifle Division, which had been at the sharp end of the German offensive:

> Enemy aviation was active using Bf 109 aircraft, which strafed with machine-gun fire and bombed our carts and vehicles carrying ammunition, as well as the approaching artillery and infantry reserves. In doing so [they created] queues at the crossroads, and at the bridges across the canals, as a result of which the normal supply of ammunition, rations and reinforcements of personnel and equipment for our troops who were advancing ahead of us, was interrupted.

However, this situation did not continue for long, and the periodical raids by fighters carrying bombs and even by FW 190 ground-attack aircraft could not inflict as much damage to Soviet supply lines as the Ju 87s and Ju 88s had done when employed extensively at the beginning of the war. They did, though, drop their bombs in a dive, which meant they could achieve a high degree of accuracy. The Red Army Air Force in Hungary remained active in the face of this *Luftwaffe* surge: on 18 January, when the Germans broke through the Soviet defenses, the crews of the 17th Air Army flew 718 mission sorties (with losses, for various reasons, of nine aircraft), and claimed the destruction or damage of 29 tanks, 191 vehicles, 72 carts and 12 railway wagons, also blowing up a warehouse and creating 54 seats of fire.

From the reports compiled by the Red Army Air Force Reconnaissance Directorate, all three of Germany's January counter-attacks that were aimed at breaking through and joining up with the encircled defenders of Budapest were supported by ground-attack and bomber aircraft. Their Ju 87s (in the first half of the month), FW 190s and less frequently He 111s in detachments of three, six and20 aircraft attacked Soviet concentrations at the bridges, as well as attacking from level flight the 3rd Ukrainian Front's formations, particularly in inclement weather conditions. Fewer raids were recorded against the neighboring 2nd Ukrainian Front, but there were reports of night bombing raids on personnel and hardware in populated areas and railway stations at Debrecen, Tiszafured and Fuzeshabol, among other locations. Soviet reports mentioned the use of Ju 88 bombers here, but the Germans usually deployed He 111s for this purpose from *KG4*, their only bomber formation, part of the I Air Corps.

Hungarian historian Ch. Sztange has put forward a theory that the Soviet Air Observation, Warning, and Communication stations and other observers mistook the Junkers for Me 210s in service with the Hungarian 102nd Dive Bombing Group (the *102 G.B.Osz*). On 19 January, the *102/2* squadron was subjected to attacks by several La-5s above Dunapentele, and one of the attacking aircraft was hit by *Unteroffizier* J. Bilau, the second victory for the *Messerschmitt* gunner. *Leutnant* M. Odescalchi shot down his 21st enemy aircraft, and the following day a group of nine Me 210s, escorted by four Bf 109s from *101/1*, destroyed an important temporary bridge across the Danube at Dunafjoldvar in a dive-bombing raid. On the same day, another formation of Me 210s went hunting for Soviet steam boats.

Despite Hungarian mobilization, the overall advantage remained with the Red Army Air Force. When the 4th Guards Army's front line was penetrated and many formations were cut off from their logistics troops, the Soviet aviation took on the job of supplying them. Invaluable assistance was provided to the troops by the 13th Medical Regiment and 14th Civilian Air Fleet Air Regiment, which formed part of the 17th Air Army. The latter unit, based 100km away from Budapest, comprised 66 aircraft in 1945 (the overwhelming majority were Po-2s, or other modifications of N.N. Polikarpov's biplane design that nevertheless had a limited power-to-weight ratio) and 103 aircrew, who had to throw themselves headlong into combat operations.

Almost all the 3rd Ukrainian Front's warehouses remained on the eastern bank of the Danube, but the bridges over the river were either blown up by the Germans or destroyed by the heavy floes of ice. The roads were difficult to traverse, making troop maneuvers more complicated, so with most of the bridges out of operation, the Soviet troops on the western bank of the Danube had to be supplied by transport

	17th Air Army			
	Type	**17 January**	**22 January**	**29 January**
Fighters	La-5	148/40	147/42	144/44
	Yak-9, Yak-3	154/30	156/31	151/40
Ground-attack aircraft	Il-2	265/33	238/30	208/40
Bombers	A-20G, B-III	97/10	89/10	66/31
Night bombers	Po-2	94/2	91/3	90/4
Reconnaissance aircraft	Pe-2	18/2	15/4	14/5
	Yak-9	8/1	6/0	4/1
Spotter aircraft	Il-2	15/1	14/2	14/1
	Yak-9	9/3	9/3	9/2
Total		**808/122**	**765/125**	**700/168**

aviation. The supply of ammunition and provisions here was almost exclusively the responsibility of the Civilian Air Fleet pilots, under Lieutenant Colonel A.I. Podsosov. "The crews in these transport aircraft fulfilled this complicated task honorably," noted a 17th Air Army report. "Flying in adverse weather conditions, by day and night, and landing exclusively among the troops in the orders of battle, often under enemy artillery, and mortar fire, they continually supplied the Army formations [under General F.G. Zakharov] with everything they needed."

Figures from 18 January, when the crews of the 17th Air Army joined the fight against the advancing tanks and mechanized infantry under *Ober-Gruppenfuhrer* Gille, who led the IV SS Panzer Corps, reveal that they flew 693 sorties, then on the following day they flew 745, on 20 January (in bad weather with thick fog) another 415, then 867 more on 21 January. By way of comparison, on these same days the Soviet Air Observation, Warning and Communication stations, according to an operational report by the General Staff, recorded flights by 300, 350, 175 and 345 enemy aircraft, respectively. Taking into consideration that some of the sorties flown by German and Hungarian aviation were made to supply the encircled Budapest garrison, the ratio of mission sorties on the outer front line of the encirclement was approximately two-to-one in favor of the Red Army Air Force.

German reports noted that on 19 January, almost all their advancing units were subject to continuous air attacks by Soviet ground-attack units escorted by fighters. This however could not inflict significant losses on the forces of the IV SS Panzer Corps. Furthermore, in many ways this undertaking was risky for the Soviet air forces themselves since in the course of the raids *Luftwaffe* fighters shot down 20 Soviet aircraft. The situation in the skies changed since significant forces from the 4th Air Fleet had been drawn up to Budapest. Their main task as before remained supply of the Hungarian capital from the air.

To ease the critical situation, the Soviet Command sent the XVIII Tank Corps, as well as units from the VII Mechanized Corps, to the threatened sector. They were joined by three rifle divisions which had been redeployed from Finland (which by this time had withdrawn from the war). They represented significant forces, but the overall plan for a Soviet counter-attack had still not materialized. Yet the Red Army reserves were far from exhausted – three additional corps (a cavalry and two mechanized corps) could also be mobilized. General Hermann Balck, commander of the German Sixth Army, in his characteristic unjustified optimism, wrote on that day: "The impression is unfolding that the enemy's principal forces are already spent." Many others, however, did not share this view, including General O. Wöhler at Army Group South, who relied on aerial reconnaissance data for a fuller picture of the strategic situation.

During those difficult days, 5th Air Army flyers of General Goryunov, in contrast to those of his 17th Air Army colleague Sudets, largely remained on the ground due to inclement weather. Among those units that were able to actively support the defenses around Székesfehérvár was the 264th Ground Attack Air Division under E.V. Klobukov. The crews of the 451st Ground Attack Air Regiment, for example, who had recently successfully completed missions to destroy encircled formations around Budapest, were now attacking columns of tanks, armored personnel carriers and vehicles from low level using anti-tank bombs. A gunner in one of the Ils, Sergeant S.A. Guryev, distinguished himself on 20 January, firing an accurate burst of fire from his UBT machine gun and setting a *Luftwaffe* ground-attack aircraft ablaze as it was coming out of its dive, which was observed by the group leader.

The Soviet General Headquarters again considered the situation on the 3rd Ukrainian Front's defensive sector to be very dangerous, and on 21 January they put the coordination of the actions of this and the 2nd Ukrainian Front in the hands of Marshal S.K. Timoshenko. (On that day alone, the 17th Air Army had lost 15 aircraft either in combat or to ground fire). On Timoshenko's instruction, a large portion of the 5th Air Army now switched over to supporting the troops that had beaten back the enemy's counter-attack on Budapest. On 22 January, using the combined forces of both the 17th and 5th Air Armies, some 1,034 sorties were completed, and according to reports by aircrew, some 36 enemy aircraft were shot down (this figure was, however, highly exaggerated). At a crucial moment, when the Germans broke through the 4th Guards Army's front line and several formations were cut off from their logistics support, transport aviation again supplied them with ammunition and organized the evacuation of the wounded. More than 500 sorties were flown in support of these stranded units.

The successful Soviet sorties helped the artillery and armored formations to maneuver around the battlefield, which together with the tenacity and courage of the infantry, and the selfless and organized maneuvers of all the units – including those that were surrounded but which continued to fight – led to the German offensive starting to wane. After having failed to reach their surrounded countrymen in the capital, the Germans were forced back onto the defensive. On 23 January, the commander of the 2nd Ukrainian Front was ordered to hand over his tank and rifle corps to the 3rd Ukrainian Front to carry out an offensive to liquidate the enemy that had broken through to the Danube, as well as to pull the 27th Army back to the front-line reserve south of Budapest, after entrusting them with the defense of Csepel Island. The responsibility for the preparation and execution of an attack from north-east of Velentse towards Sharoshde was entrusted to Marshal Tolbukhin.

Meantime, after crossing the road to Budapest, the Germans broke through the defenses of the cavalry group under General S.I. Gorshkov, while German tanks even forced their way through to the artillery positions of the 877th Howitzer Artillery Regiment. They also succeeded in flanking the stronghold of Barachka. The SS forces, however, still could not take Barachka. The main role in beating back the German attacks here was played by Soviet aviation. The commander of the V Guards Cavalry Corps later even wrote a note of thanks to the pilots of the 136th Ground Attack Air Division under Colonel N.P. Terekhov:

> On that difficult day on 25 January, when a crisis emerged in the battle for Barachka, a tipping point in the battle in our favor was brought about by the '*ilyushins*' that appeared over the battlefield. Despite the adverse weather conditions – falling snow and limited visibility – the bombing was exceptionally accurate and the pilots put an end to a decisive attack by enemy tanks. All the Cossacks, the sergeants, officers, and generals in the Cossack Corps are delighted with your work on 25 January 1945.

TA counter-attack by the XXIII Tank Corps of the 2nd Ukrainian Front was unsuccessful and ended in significant losses. The pilots of the 10thGround Attack Air Corps operated energetically on 25 January in the area around Barachka. Some 58 Il-2s flew 164 sorties that day, or three sorties a day by the majority of the corps' combat-capable aircraft, a high intensity of combat. Losses were insignificant – just one Il-2 was shot down by Axis anti-aircraft artillery crews. Overall, though, the Germans could be pleased here with the success of their actions, having achieved a specific success with the IV SS Panzer Corps breaking out across a narrow front from the defile between Lake Velentse and the Danube. However, it was was to be their final major success.

Although the attacking German foces were now only 25–30km from the Budapest garrison, their commanders understood how slim their chances were of achieving a decisive breakthrough to the capital, given the unfolding situation elsewhere. The *Luftwaffe* and their Hungarian allies, though, did all they could to assist the offensive. According to a report from the Air Defense System Directorate of the 3rd Ukrainian Front, the Germans made the most powerful air attacks on the 4th Guards Army positions on 16 January, with some 172 bombers or ground-attack aircraft participating in seven raids. The neighboring Soviet 46th Army was also subjected to powerful attacks on 21 January (177 air strikes) and 23 January (167 air strikes). The same report also reveals that the Soviet front-line logistics were not subjected to air attacks, that the German pilots were able to regroup without any interruption from Soviet and Hungarian aviation, and that the aircraft of the 141st Air Defense System Fighter Air Division – which had been tasked with covering the Ukrainian fronts' logistics – all but sat idly on their aerodromes at this time. Moreover, the Soviet fighter pilots hardly even got airborne to chase the German and Hungarian reconnaissance aircraft which flew regular missions in the area.

Throughout the German attempts to break through to Budapest, the anti-aircraft crews of the Soviet 9th Anti-Aircraft Artillery Division under Colonel N.A. Roshchitskiy fired either at group targets (made up of three or four aircraft) or individual aircraft. They shot down 10 enemy aircraft, predominantly FW 190s. The 22nd Anti-Aircraft Artillery Division, meanwhile, enjoyed similar results during the defense of the crossings at Dunapentele and in beating back attacks by *panzer* formations south of Székesfehérvár. On more than one occasion, the anti-aircraft artillery crews fired at ground targets and defended themselves with rifle fire from groups of German machine gunners who had infiltrated their firing positions. In land battles, the regiments of the 22nd Division under the recently promoted Major General I.M. Danshin destroyed eight tanks, six armored transporters and eight other vehicles, suppressed fire from seven guns and killed or wounded more than 1,000 enemy officers and other ranks.

The Red Army Air Force was active operationally on 29 January. Despite snowfall, thick cloud cover and cold weather (thermometers dropped to -8°C by day), the aircraft of the 3rd Ukrainian Front flew 950 mission sorties, including 326 at night. In 12 air battles, nine German aircraft were shot down (a further two were hit by anti-aircraft artillery crews), while 23 enemy tanks, four armored personnel carriers, 123 other vehicles, 41 carts, five field artillery guns and 10 anti-aircraft guns were either destroyed or damaged. Two Axis ammunition stores were blown up, creating up to 50 islands of fire, and setting off four large explosions. The pilots in Sudets' 17th Air Army alone destroyed almost 60 buildings in Budapest which had been converted into enemy strongholds. In response, the German and Hungarian aviation flew, according to the Soviet Air Observation, Warning, and Communication stations, 135 sorties, of which 49 were transport sorties.

According to Soviet data, their losses here were low: two La-5s were hit by anti-aircraft fire, and two Il-2s and a single Boston failed to return from their mission. There were, however, non-combat losses: one of the most successful aces in the 17th Air Army and in the Red Army Air Force as a whole, Hero of the Soviet Union Major N.F. Krasnov from the 530th Fighter Air Regiment – who had shot down 40 enemy aircraft individually, with one shared victory, including four on 22 January 1945 – was killed. Another Soviet ace, Major N.M. Skomorokhov, who served in the 31st Fighter Air Regiment and whom Krasnov considered his mentor in the techniques of air combat and leadership skills, recalled how on take-off, the left undercarriage leg had failed to retract on Krasnov's aircraft, then the Lavochkin's engine began to misfire, after which it stopped and the pilot was forced to make an emergency landing.

Skomorokhov later wrote of the entire sequence of unfortunate circumstances on that day which led to Krasnov's demise:

> Krasnov saw a smooth-looking field below him, where our downed Boston had already landed. On landing the Lavochkin rolled over onto its back and lay there with the cockpit facing downwards. Nikolay Fyodorovich Krasnov, who had been knocked unconscious by the impact, was hanging there in the straps. His wingman, instead of landing on his belly alongside the aircraft, returned to base from where a Po-2 was dispatched, but this aircraft got lost. A technician who had been standing guard over the Boston ran up to help, crawling under the overturned fighter. He could see that the pilot could be pulled clear, but only by breaking the fuselage in two, and ran off to the nearest village in search of an axe. While all this was happening, Major Krasnov passed away.

The end of the month passed with Soviet aviators now enjoying the distinct upper hand, something, which the Germans were in no position to challenge, and Operation *Konrad-3* having failed. Taking stock of the situation, the 17th Air Army headquarters noted:

> In the course of the Budapest Operation in severe battles with a numerically superior enemy, and in exceptionally inclement weather conditions, and difficult circumstances with respect to the network of aerodromes, 17th Air Army units supported ground forces, successfully destroying the enemy, whilst offering support to troops and mobile formations. The skilful and decisive actions of our ground-attack aircraft, bombers and fighters destroyed tanks, artillery, vehicular transport, and enemy aircraft, and killed enemy personnel. There were days when the enemy refused to attack ground targets in daylight, citing heavy losses at the hands of our aircraft. Our fighters actively destroyed enemy aircraft in the air, preventing mass enemy air raids against our ground troops and their orders of battle, and restricting any interdiction by enemy fighter aviation against our ground-attack aircraft, and bombers.

At the same time, however, the significant successes enjoyed by the units of the German 4th Air Fleet in the January battles also has to be acknowledged. They flew more than 7,500 mission sorties, or more than 300 per day when there was good weather. German fighters claimed 395 victories along the entire Soviet–German front, of which 210 (or 53 percent) were attained by Colonel General O. Dessloch's 4th Air Fleet. The Soviet 8th Air Army of the 4th Ukrainian Front incurred insignificant losses in air battles, and the 5th Air Army some small losses, predominantly during the air blockade of Budapest, but the 17th Air Army suffered a great deal and it was against this group that the *Messerschmitt* pilots subordinate to *St./JG76*, concentrated their main efforts. If German claims are to be believed, then every 10th sortie by their fighter pilots ended in the destruction of a Soviet aircraft, whilst they incurred just one loss themselves in every 44 sorties. Whilst German ground-attack aircraft were more rarely active, of the 4,151 sorties flown, the pilots of *SG2*'s 10 squadrons claimed 28 Soviet aircraft shot down, mainly Il-2s, at the price of 48 of their own aircraft.

The primary burden of the battle was borne, unsurprisingly, by the Hungarian *101.V.* fighter regiment under Major A. de Heppesze, which was subordinated to 76th Squadron headquarters, as were the German air groups; the squadron claimed 69 enemy aircraft shot down (different sources put this number at 49). The fighter unit completed around 400 mission sorties and they lost 14 aircraft shot down, while 15 sustained various degrees of damage; seven pilots were either killed or missing without trace. The *II/JG52* group fought with some success, claiming 44 aircraft shot down (seven of its pilots were either killed or missing without trace), and the most successful German ace in January was H. Ewald, who scored 18 victories.

In January, the Soviet 17th Air Army lost 348 aircraft (37 percent of the number they started with), of which 295 were shot down in air battles or by anti-aircraft fire. The Chief of Staff, Major General N.M. Korkasov, in his closing report, divided the Soviet mistakes and oversights that had led to these sad results into tactical and organizational categories. He put the tactical losses down to poor organization of defensive fire in the groups of fighters and ground-attack aircraft, and the fragmentation of formations during the course of an air battle and when breaking away from the target. He also cited the frequent organization of attack aircraft into a pattern, when 12, 18 or 24 ground-attack aircraft and bombers were escorted by four to six fighters without taking into account the actual situation in the air, as well as aircraft being dispatched forward too early and the sending of patrols of large numbers of aircraft to the battlefield to search for enemy 'hunters'. He put the organizational losses down to poor headquarters briefings to aircrew of the actual situation in the air, poor organization of flight operations – which led to delays in the established timescales for groups of aircraft to meet up in the air – the fact that these were unnecessarily long and the rare employment of mass raids on the enemy, which could have put a stop to the losses.

The report also highlighted the inaccurate detailed orientation of the area over the target by the leading groups, the deployment of AO-25 and FAB-50 aerial bombs against well-armored tanks (allegedly capable of hitting them with a blast wave or shrapnel), the raising of the altitude at which Aerial Anti-Tank Bombs (PTAB) were dropped by two or three times above the optimal altitude (100–200m), as a result of which they would scatter over a wide area, and using a single approach for ground attacks. This meant that only a small amount of the armament on an Il-2 was used, which while not linked to an increase in Soviet losses, reduced the effect of the action on the enemy. Sorties by groups of aircraft (recorded in relation to the 189th Ground Attack Air Division and 194th Fighter Air Division) without taking into account the meteorological situation led to bitter losses of matériel and in some cases of crews.

The 10thGround Attack Air Corps suffered terribly in January as never before, losing 208 aircraft. A report written by O.V. Tolstikov, who served in this formation, stated that in the course of its sorties the enemy would attack the Il-2s more than once in an encounter battle, positioning themselves slightly above the aircraft they were attacking, and that these attacks were predominantly made by FW 190 ground-attack aircraft. Since they were well armored and had a powerful engine, individual pilots would usually approach Soviet aircraft from behind and slightly above, while another detachment would attack from above and in front almost at the same time. In many cases this tactic, which was based on the element of surprise, did bring the Germans success. The fitting of many Bf 109s with 30mm MK 108 guns also played a role. While in the course of 1943 the Corps (up until 29 September 1944 it was known as the IX Mixed Corps) flew 17,401 sorties and lost 299 aircraft, the following year it flew 20,740 sorties and lost 184 aircraft, and in 1945 the figures were 17,303 sorties with 246 aircraft lost.

The Soviets' new Romanian allies also had some serious challenges ahead. In the first few days of 1945, their I Air Corps was active for the most part on the left flank of the 2nd Ukrainian Front and against the encircled forces in Budapest. However, from the beginning of Operation *Konrad-3*, the Romanians supported the 17th Air Army (notably with Hs 129 ground-attack and Ju 87 dive-bomber aircraft, which were now active against the nation that had produced them). During sorties on the external front in the battles against German and Hungarian formations near Budapest, Romanian losses were significant, and sometimes huge. According to the memoirs of General V.A. Kuznetsov, who at that time was a senior lieutenant, the Deputy Squadron Commander of the 122nd Fighter Air Regiment (V Ground Attack Corps) once made an emergency landing on the section of an aerodrome occupied by the Soviets, on which Soviet ground-attack aircraft stood alongside Yaks, in a Ju 87 damaged by shrapnel and wearing Romanian markings.

Throwing up his hands in sorrow, the Romanian pilot said: "The fascists shot down seven of our aircraft; I was the only one left." He went on to describe what had happened in the air, gesticulating energetically with his hands:

> By chance, as we were flying westwards, a group of eight [of our] Ju 87s were met by 10 Fw 190s. The Germans were heading east to provide air cover over the battlefield. We rocked our wings and went off in different directions. They thought we were German, as we were flying Junkers aircraft! We bombed the German column and set off back to base. That was when it all happened ... The leader of the German group drew closer to the 'eighty-sevens', saw the Romanian Air Force markings, and ordered the attack. The Ju 87s began to fall towards the ground.

The Commander of the Soviet 5th Air Army, General S.K. Goryunov.

After failed plot of 20 July 1944, Heinz Guderian was appointed Chief of the General Staff of the Army and was commanding during the defense of Hungary.

A Soviet observer in a clock tower in the central part of Pest adjusts artillery fire as well as ground-attack aircraft operations.

A view of the Danube at the beginning of the ice flow, taken from a reconnaissance aircraft, in December 1944.

Ground-attack aircraft from the 17th Air Army on a forward airfield south of Budapest.

Aerial view of Budapest at the end of 1944, shortly before the assault. :

Soviet technician adjusting the M-11 engine of the Po-2 airplane, 17th Air Army.

An 88mm gun and an armoured personnel carrier that were destroyed on a Budapest street by anti-tank bombs dropped by Soviet ground-attack aircraft.

Li-2 aircraft from the V Long-Range Air Corps deliver much-needed cargoes to forward units in the area around the Danube.

An Me 210 fighter-bomber manufactured in Hungary on the edge of an airfield in December 1944.

A squadron of Il-2 aircraft built with the funds collected by workers of Volsk town in Saratov region. In the foreground, Professor A.M. Predchetenskiy, an initiator of the funds collection, is listening to the pilot's explanations.

Technicians cover the engine of a ground-attack aircraft for the night to keep its oil warm.

Assembly of an Il-2 at factory No. 30 by Viktor Yermilov's (right) Brigade. The Soviet front needed thousands of new aircraft.

Technicians carry a container for attaching under Hs.129B-2. Note 30-mm belly-mounted cannon.

A group of ground crews (aircraft and engine technicians) of the 235th ShAP in front of the combat aircraft.

Assembly of new Bf.109G fighters at the factory in Wiener Neustadt.

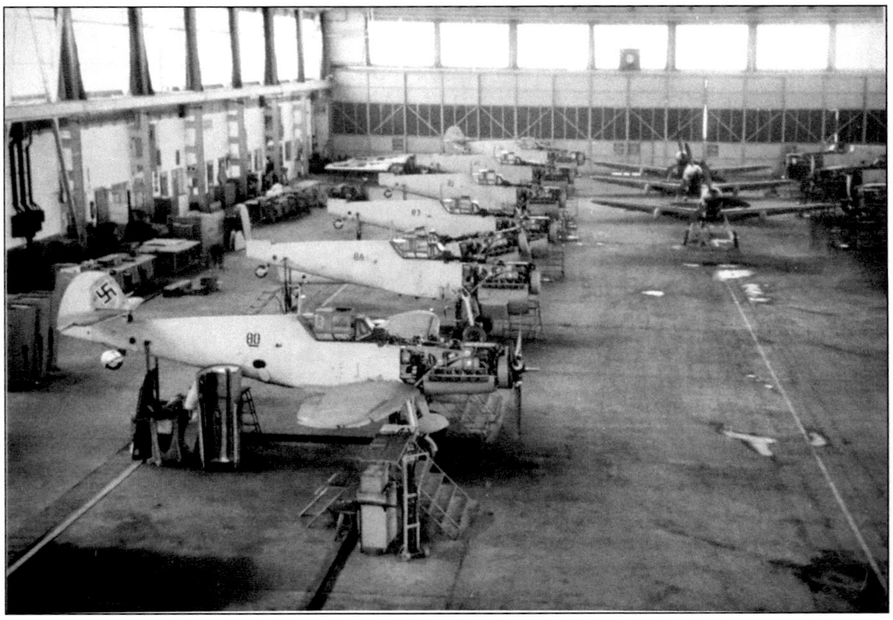

6

Blockade

In an attempt to avoid bloodshed, the Soviet high command sent the encircled forces in Budapest an ultimatum on 29 January that proposed humane terms for surrender for the officers and men of the garrison. However, envoys Hungarian Captain M. Shteimnetz and Ukrainian Captain I.A. Ostapenko, who were sent across the German lines as envoys under flags of truce, were both killed in circumstances that remain unclear. Without prior knowledge of this act, 707th Ground Attack Air Regiment (189th Ground Attack Air Division) pilots Senior Lieutenant N.A. Shmelev and Junior Lieutenant P.I. Orlov, in inclement weather with poor visibility and snow showers, dropped 1.5 million leaflets across the city at low altitude providing details of the Soviet ultimatum.

The anti-aircraft defenses of Budapest were strong, with the exception of night fighters. In order to discover the whereabouts of anti-aircraft artillery and searchlight stations, Soviet crews would fly several sorties in reasonable weather conditions, after which an evaluation was made at headquarters based on their reports. They discovered that the city was defended by seven or eight medium-caliber anti-aircraft batteries and no more than 14 small-caliber batteries (including multi-barrel guns) – in total at least 200 guns – plus between 15 and 18 powerful searchlights. These represented the principal forces of the 15th German Motorized Anti-Aircraft Division. How strong their anti-aircraft fire was across the city is highlighted in the memoirs of Captain V.A. Kuznetsov of 122nd Fighter Air Regiment (V Ground Attack Air Corps), who often flew reconnaissance sorties at the time in his Yak:

> The ground-attack aircraft [fly] over Budapest. The fascists do not give up, even though they are being bombed and strafed: There were no enemy aircraft in the skies, and we would be able to easily observe the Hungarian capital: the grey apartment blocks, mostly on the left, eastern bank of the Danube, the straight streets and the beautiful bridges cast across the enormous span of the river. On the western bank there were far fewer apartment blocks ... the anti-aircraft crews are constantly firing. Well, let them fire. They have to fire between 2,000 and 3,000 shells to shoot an aircraft down. So you maneuver once, then again and you no longer fear the anti-aircraft crews. While the Ils were dropping their bombs it was time to descend and take our photographs. There were no enemy fighters around, and we made it easily back to Jaszbereny [east of the capital]."

Senior Lieutenant G.P. Yevdokimov of the 449th Bomber Air Regiment, who was one of the first to strike the defenders after the encirclement had been closed, recalled:

> The decisive moment was coming closer, which was why the group had arrived here. As you approached the city from the air the bridges across the Danube and the hills of Buda become more and more clearly discernable. The calculations had been done and the information fed to the sights. The only thing left to do was look for the target. The city was bristling with a dense wall of fire: they were firing in Buda and in Pest. One got the impression that the only people left in the city were the anti-aircraft crews.
>
> Everything around had already turned into a ring of fire – this was a familiar and unpleasant sight, one it was impossible to get used to. A phrase that I had read once passed through my mind: they have to fire 600 shells to shoot down one aircraft. How many had they fired at us?! To tell the truth, I had got fed up with them. I just had to find and hit the target. The group, maneuvering on a heading, was approaching the start of their approach (the southern bridge across the Danube). I could see the fortress and the fortress ramparts. Our target should be 300m beyond the contours of the wall. I imagined this location in my mind. All my thoughts were focused on it. The bomb bay doors were open – the group had started its approach.

Looking at events from the defenders' perspective, Hungarian historian P. Postoni noted: "One of the most inherent concerns for those in the encirclement from the very first day of the blockade was supplying the city, which was made all the more difficult by the fact that around 800,000 civilian residents remained in the city, aside from the military, and they were not ready at all for a protracted blockade. From the very beginning, however, it was clear that supplying the city with provisions and ammunition by air would not be sufficient to meet the needs of the encircled troops. Hitler had entrusted the 4th Air Fleet with the immediate organization of supplies by air. The daily volume of cargoes required by Army Group South for the fortress was more than 80 tons, this for the most part beding made up of ammunition, fuel, provisions, and medical supplies.

The Germans were very efficient in organizing supplies for the encircled garrison, the Luftwaffe having amassed an enormous amount of experience in setting up 'air bridges' by the end of 1944. On 29 December, the transport air command 'Budapest' was established under Generalleutnant G. Konrad, forming part of the 4th Air Fleet. This was initially made up of the III/TG2 under Major J. Penkert and the II/TG3 (not long before these events, an aircraft carrying its commander, Major G. Dudeck, had disappeared over Macedonia and he was taken prisoner, but a successor had not been appointed), with reinforcement detachments. That same day, the first 'auntie Jus' (as the Germans dubbed the three-engine Hugo Junkers-designed Ju 52 transport aircraft) arrived in Budapest.

The Luftwaffe's 4th Bomber Squadron was destined to play an important role in the defence of Budapest. The headquarters and the I/KG4 'General Wefer' was at that time based on the Novy Dvor aerodrome in Slovakia, near the Hungarian border, while the II/KG4 was atthe Wiener-Neustadt aerodrome not far from Vienna. Both units spent time idle owing to a lack of fuel, but at the height of the crisis in Hungary they were allocated the required reserves from the special 'Fuhrer's reserve'. On 23 December, Heinkels bombed the Soviet troop positions around the city, while on the night of 24/25 December they attacked the crossing point across the Danube near Dunafjoldvar. On the final day of 1944, the 4th Bomber Squadron – under its commodore Major R. Graubner, who until recently had been a squadron leader – had 54 bombers, of which 29 were combat-ready.

Shortly after the start of the transportation of supplies into Budapest, the I/TG3 Air Group was drafted into the operation, as well as the I/LLG2 paratrooper Air Group and Hungarian transport squadrons. The Germans had no way to be certain that these forces would be sufficient, since aside from military personnel the city was still home to more than three-quarters of a million civilians. At the beginning of January 1945, the III/KG4 under Major G. von Kruzki arrived at Wiener-Neustadt. Thus the whole 'General Wefer' squadron had come together again for the first time since Operation Frogspawn – the mining of navigation channels near Kronstadt and Leningrad between May and June 1942 – which was a landmark moment for its personnel! As the distance from their base to Budapest was not very far, and the requirements of the pocket far outweighed the capabilities of German and Hungarian transport aviation, the pilots operated under considerable pressure, sometimes flying two or three sorties a night (they now had around 50 serviceable He 111s).

In the first days of the new year, the principal forces of the Soviet 17th Air Army had still not been transferred to supporting the troops who were stubbornly fighting to the north-west of the capital, continuing to batter the encircled Axis forces. "Looking through the 31st Regiment's Combat Journal, I was struck by the number of sorties and the variety of the missions," recalled one of the best aces of the entire 17th Air Army, Major N.M. Skomorokhov. On the first page of his journal there is an abbreviated entry:

> 2 January 1945 1245–1340. Four of Kravtsov's La-5s (Junior Lieutenants Tsykin, Popov and Kalinin). Escorting an Il-2 close to Budapest. A group of Il-2s attacked four pairs of FW 190s. The victories were as follows: Junior Lieutenant Popov – one FW 190; Junior Lieutenant Kalinin – one FW 190; Major Kravtsov – a Bf 109 and an FW 190. Major Kravstov failed to return from his sortie.

For two days there was no information on the fate of Dmitri Stepanovich Kravtsov, before it emerged that Soviet troops had picked him up, and as he was in a critical condition they sent him to hospital. Escorting the ground-attack aircraft alone, Major Kravtsov had not allowed the Focke-Wulfs to strafe or shoot them down at close range with impunity, but communication was lost with his wingman, who was distracted by an air battle. After this clash, in which the enemy's bursts of gunfire set his Lavochkin on fire and hit Kravtsov's leg and arm, he was out of action for some considerable time. Squadron commander Kravtsov had attained 13 personal victories and eight shared victories. Soon after these events, the commander of the 31st Fighter Air Regiment, Major G.D. Onufrienko, signed a document recommending his subordinate for the title of Hero of the Soviet Union.

The principal elements of 5th Air Army were also directed towards supporting Lieutenant General I.M. Managarov's Budapest Group, which had been tasked with purging Budapest of Hungarian and German forces as quickly as possible. The commander of the III Guards Fighter Air Corps, General I.D. Podgorny, sent all three divisions (the 6th, 13th and 14th Guards Fighter Air Divisions) to patrol over the city and occasionally carry out ground-attack raids on targets they identified. The report of the 5th Air Army indicated the significant assistance the pilots in Goryunov's Army offered to the ground forces in their fighting for the city and its surroundings:

> Over the course of 2 January 1945 pilots [from this formation alone] flew 982 mission sorties to perform their combat objectives, of which 628 were for bombing and ground-attack missions against personnel and military hardware. Despite the powerful resistance from enemy anti-aircraft fire the crews destroyed five armored personnel carriers, 97 vehicles [– the vehicle fleet at Keleti station was almost completely destroyed by a group of Il-2s, led by the commander of the 235th Ground Attack Air Regiment, Lieutenant Colonel A.V. Bezdenechnykh –], fire from four field batteries and three anti-aircraft artillery batteries was suppressed, and hundreds of enemy officers and men were killed.

Late on the evening of 2 January, German aircraft were particularly active in supplying the embattled defenders of Budapest and evacuating the wounded on their return flights, together with anything of material value. The Soviet 60th Separate Searchlight Company, which had arrived the previous day to augment the 9th Anti-Aircraft Artillery Division with five searchlights, was particularly opportune in its arrival in the suburbs; on the night of 2/3 January, the detachment was set to work in this area for the first time, capturing 10 transport aircraft in their searchlights. However, not one of them was shot down or seriously damaged by Soviet pilots or anti-aircraft crews.

Successful development of the Soviet offensive led to the loss of most of the fully equipped aerodromes in Budaors (which had three large hangars, good railway access and stationary anti-aircraft batteries that were abandoned during the German withdrawal), Ferihendi and Matyashfyorde. On 3 January, the Red Army approached the racecourse and the landing strip on Csepel Island, after making a dangerous landing on the island. The German 4th Air Army Command then gathered up to 100 light, three- or four-seat courier or Fi 156 communication aircraft from different departments and flying schools, which were able to land on very short runways, including city streets and squares. These aircraft were used to evacuate the wounded, and subsequently the glider pilots (on occasion along with their gliders, when the landing had been a successful one, without any incident or collision with obstructions).

As noted by F. Morzik, the inspector general of Luftwaffe transport aviation, who was the author of a series of historical works, the I/LLG2 parachute assault group was initially not able to operate in its standard configuration: the Do 17 towing aircraft did not have the special rigid couplings fitted, which meant it was impossible to use the 'sky trains' at night, and the pilots were not experienced in flying in darkness. Several He 111 and KG4 bombers were converted to transport the DFS 230 gliders, and Ju 87s later began to be used from the groups of night bombers. This, however, was only possible after additional training.

Hungarian aviation also played its part in supplying the garrison, allocating around 20 transport aircraft to this task, predominantly Ju 52s. The number of flights made by their crews to the city was small compared to their German counterparts, which can be explained by the low level of serviceability of their aircraft, as well as the need to fulfill other tasks. Apart from that, the will to fight among the Hungarians was significantly less by this time than that of their German allies. Incidents of defection to the Soviets were not infrequent. On 6 January 1945, Captain W. Stifler deliberately changed course mid-flight, after which he and three other Hungarian aviators landed on an aerodrome south of the city of Solnok. These pilots were undoubtedly acting in accordance with a pre-arranged plan.

During interrogation at the 2nd Ukrainian Front headquarters, Stifler spoke for the most part about the participation of Hungarian aviation in supplying the Budapest garrison. Up until 25 December, two Hungarian squadrons, which had been amalgamated into a special transport group under the General Headquarters, had 12 Ju 52 aircraft based at Budaors, which were subsequently transferred to Pápa. Losses amounted to five aircraft: one was shot down by Soviet fighters near Esztergom, one fell victim to accurate artillery fire over Budapest racecourse and another two met with accidents following their redeployment to Pápa (the fifth aircraft was the one flown by Stifler). Stifler added:

> When Budapest had still not been encircled the German–Hungarian Command made sufficiently wide use of transport aviation to supply the garrison, as well as the city's population with provisions, landing in Budaors, and flying by day at low level; now they fly at night, landing on the territory of the racecourse or on Csepel Island. According to German acquaintances transport aviation suffered the greatest losses from mortar fire on the runway."

The Soviet 5th, 9th and 38th Anti-Aircraft Artillery Divisions enforced the blockade, along with two separate anti-aircraft artillery regiments, which enabled a high intensity of fire. After the German forces had gone on the offensive from the Komarno region, however, the anti-aircraft artillery defences west of Budapest had to be weakened, transferring units from the 9th Division to augment the air defenses of the 46th Army. Cooperation between Soviet formations at the beginning of January was poor, while reconnaissance of the enemy's air forces using radar stations was inadequate and anti-aircraft battery maneuvers were restricted by them being few in number and by the high degree of wear in their vehicles and artillery tractors.

According to Soviet documents, the Air Observation, Warning and Communication stations were able to identify in relatively good weather some 40–50 flights each day by transport aircraft, of which half were across the 46th Army's battle lines (in heavy cloud cover it was not possible to keep tabs on them), while fewer instances of landings in the besieged city were recorded. In the meantime, the Red Army's ground-attack groups were constantly purging the city; by 5 January, 254 blocks in the city had been occupied, predominantly in Peshte. Among the prized Soviet captures was the Messerchmitt engine factory, the radio plant in the east of the city and warehouses that were full of various items of radio equipment for aircraft, guided bombs, and tanks.

The Germans and Hungarians continued to stubbornly hold the most important sites in the city, and went on the offensive themselves more than once, so it was not clear how long their forces could hold out. The IX SS Mountain Rifle Corps continued to send anxious and at times desperate telegrams to the headquarters of Army Group South: "If airborne supplies do not start soon then ammunition for the machine guns, mortars and field guns will only last until 9 January, and other ammunition only until 12 January, food and fuel will last until 10 January, and provisions until 11 January. There are 3,880 wounded in Budapest, of which 1,400 are seriously wounded. The situation requires an immediate solution."

The Soviet Command took steps to try to break the enemy's will to fight as quickly as possible, including a decision to introduce Romanian aviation into the battle. On 12 January, eight IAR-81 aircraft were redeployed to Debrecen to augment the air defenses around the city, although this was of minimal benefit. By day, Boston aircraft were used, which for all their advantages were not able to effectively hit small targets that were heavily protected by anti-aircraft guns. The anti-aircraft defense of Budapest – where the Germans had sent a significant proportion of their batteries from the 15th Motorized Anti-Aircraft Artillery Division – still represented a powerful force. When on the following day, the commander of the 17th Romanian Dive-Bomber Squadron, Lieutenant Badulescu, led a group of seven Ju 87D-5s in a raid on Budapest, he experienced the full force of his former ally's air defenses.

The target was the Elizabeth (Erzsebet) Bridge, which was the main transport artery linking Buda and Pest and well defended by various anti-aircraft guns. Soviet bombers had made several attempts to destroy this bridge, deploying fragmentation ordnance, but they were unable to interrupt movements across it. It was now the turn of the Romanians to demonstrate their skills. After climbing to an altitude of 4,000m, the dive-bombers met their escorts on their approach to the city and were joined by Soviet Yaks. When the Romanian and Soviet pilots dive-bombed the bridge, it initially appeared that the strike had been successful – four bombs hit the main span and only one aircraft was struck by ground fire, and the pilot was still able to land his aircraft on the nearest 'friendly' aerodrome. The bridge, however, continued to function. The next strike on the bridge was made by four Ju 88As that remained in Romanian service. Gheorghe Georgescu (a very experienced pilot, who during the course of the war had flown around 200 mission sorties) led this raid. Before they reached the target, though, one of the Junkers had to return to base as its worn-out engine failed. The remaining trio of aircraft attacked the bridge from an altitude of 5,000m. After descending to 1,500m, they released their 250kg bombs, at least two of which hit the road over the bridge. Despite heavy anti-aircraft fire, all three aircraft made it back to base. The bridge survived the attack but was blown up by the Germans a few days later on 18 January.

The Germans realized the Red Army Air Force and that of its allies were targeting the capital's crucial bridges, and on 13 January, a message was sent from the IX SS Mountain Rifle Corps to the headquarters of Army Group South confirming the success of the raids in curtailing the movement of troops over the Danube:

> The battle for Budapest has reached its apogee. The eastern stronghold is subject to constant attacks with powerful artillery, fighter aviation and tank support ... In the daytime, movement around the city is paralyzed by constant air attacks, which are directed first and foremost at the bridges across the Danube. Several of them have been seriously damaged. It is anticipated that shortly after 15 January the eastern stronghold [the positions in Pest] will be lost.

The German Command devoted a great deal of attention to the retention of the bridges since their presence enabled their reserves to maneuver and made it much easier to hold together an unfragmented front. Some of the more experienced Soviet pilots specifically tried to destroy the bridges. Lieutenant G.P. Odnotsenov, for example, of the 951st Ground Attack Air Regiment (who by the beginning of 1945 had flown more than 100 successful Il-2 sorties), was given a specific order by 17th Air Army commander General Sudets to destroy or damage the bridges as much as possible. From 11–14 January, Odnotsenov flew 17 sorties, and maneuvering skillfully under strong anti-aircraft fire, he achieved seven direct hits, destroying two spans. It is known that the Horthy Miklos Bridge was destroyed on 15 January, while late in the evening of 16 January, a heavy bomb blew up the Franz-Joszef Bridge.

To the defender's astonishment, several Soviet fighters appeared over the city with bombs under their wings. The 194th Fighter Air Division had been given a new objective, which was set out in the following report:

> From the beginning of 1945, training for the Division's units in carrying out bombing attacks began. This training for the most part encompassed detailed study of quarters of the city, large, standalone buildings, and characteristic landmarks on a street plan, and also using photographs obtained from the reconnaissance section of the 17th Air Army headquarters. In addition a series of measures were taken to study the control of fighters over the battlefield and the organization of their cooperation with ground forces. After liberating the commanding height 529.0 located 3 kilometers west of the city of Budapest, a ground based radio guidance system was mounted, and a senior aviation commander was permanently stationed there [divisional commander Colonel F.N. Dementyev] ... bombing using La-5 and La-7 aircraft has been carried out in a dive of between 60° and 65° from altitudes of between 1,200m and 1,500m using FAB-100 or FAB-50 bombs.

The storming of Budapest was undertaken with active air support, particularly from Soviet ground-attack aircraft. Lieutenant Colonel B.N. Yeremin, deputy commander of the 6th Guards Fighter Air Division, who personally participated in directing the attack aircraft to the target while the pilots of his division were covering them from the air, reported:

> Despite the difficulties of orientation in this large city, the ground-attack aircraft pilots made what were sniper-like attacks on the enemy's strongholds. This effective work by the ground-attack aircraft was made possible by the cooperation of aviation with ground forces. In the course of the battles the situation in one or other district of the city was changing every day on an hourly basis. When the next group of Il-2s arrived, the situation for our forces was communicated to them from the ground using rockets. For the most part however the accuracy of the attacks by the ground-attack aircraft depended on the precise work of the aviation representatives, and forward air controllers, supported by the pilots flying their fighter escorts.

The German 4th Air Fleet Command, meanwhile, did not stop their flights from the pocket, but Army Group South always kept the issue of the number of transport aircraft sent to Budapest under control. It was just that there was no 'feedback' as such – nobody knew in detail how much in terms of cargo had been taken to the encircled troops. The weather conditions exacerbated the situation regarding resupply of the garrison. There was heavy snowfall in Austria in mid-January, and in two days Wiener-Neustadt aerodrome was covered in a layer of snow almost a meter thick. Luftwaffe technical personnel were joined by pilots in clearing snow from the runways to a length of 900m and a width of 300m. Even the headquarters officers and the commander of II/KG54, Major Hesse, took up a shovel. After two days of uninterrupted work, flights to Budapest resumed.

Fierce aerial battles often ensued when Soviet pilots intercepted aircraft that were flying into the pocket. Overall, Soviet losses were somewhat higher, both in terms of aircraft and personnel: many Soviet aces perished just a few months short of final victory. Others had close friends who fell or were reported missing without trace. On 16 January, Soviet pilots intercepted groups of – as well as individual – German transport aircraft flying cargoes to the encircled troops; according to Red Army Air Force records, they shot down 17 Ju 52s. On that day, Junior Lieutenant A.K. Buykevich of the 659th Fighter Air Regiment (288th Fighter Air Division, 17th Air Army) and leading aces Captains K.A. Yevstigneyev of the 178th Guards Fighter Air Regiment (III Guards Fighter Air Corps, 5th Air Army) and N.M. Skomorokhov of the 31st Fighter Air Regiment (259th Fighter Air Division, 17th Air Army) each scored two transport aircraft in their tally. Nikolay Mikhaylovich Skomorokhov lost his leading wingman Junior Lieutenant I.F. Filippov, who had selflessly gone to his assistance in battle on more than one occasion. After returning from a successful sortie, he dived into thick smoke that was rising up from the riverr, reached the Danube and hurriedly looked for somewhere to land, anxious to discuss with his colleague the ups and downs of the day:

> I could not see him anymore. He appeared over the aerodrome with just one undercarriage leg deployed. He did not try to land – he initiated a go around. After that he disappeared forever, he vanished into obscurity. We waited for him to return until late into the evening, we waited the next day and on the third. We actively searched for him – we covered the entire area around the aerodrome. [and] with the help of divers we searched several sections of the Danube. We found wreckage from his Lavochkin, and established his registration, but it did not fit with I.F. Filippov's logbook. Thus even today we still do not know what happened to him, but everyone had come to the conclusion that Junior Lieutenant Ivan Filippovich Filippov had vanished under the Danube's waves."

According to German records, a group consisting of 25 He 111s, escorted by Messerschmitts, was subjected to powerful attacks from Soviet fighters on their way to the encircled forces on 16 January. The Germans claimed they had shot down 16 aircraft with red stars on their sides. However, other records estimate that only seven or eight Soviet fighters failed to return from their missions, of which five belonged to the 288th Fighter Air Division. It emerged the following day that Senior Lieutenant M.A. Fisenko and his wingman Junior Lieutenant N.I. Galkin, of the 659th Fighter Air Regiment, had been killed, but a flight of Yak-3s from the 897th Fighter Air Regiment, having used up all their fuel in flight, had landed at Madoche aerodrome, returning safely to their unit the following day. Thus, Soviet losses did not exceed five fighters.

The Germans lost at least 10 or 12 aircraft in these clashes, including one Bf 109G from II/JG52 and two FW 190Fs from III/SG10, which failed to return from their sorties. Consequently, on that day the Red Army Air Force got the better of their adversaries. In an evening battle, two Ju 52/3ms were shot down – W.No. 5441 (10/TG2) and W.No. 641033 (5/TG2) – although several Junkers aircraft were seriously damaged. On 16 January, the KG4 squadron lost four aircraft, including Ober-Feldwebel Wiesenpfarth's crew, who along with their experienced radio-operator Feldwebel Saalfrank had flown more than 100 sorties behind enemy lines. The reason for the loss of the crew, as given in a report, was a collision with the ground in inclement weather near to the Little Carpathians aerodrome. As had been the case with flights into the Stalingrad pocket in the winter of 1942/43, German crews would often make deliberate use of poor weather to avoid interception in the air.

Leonid Pervomayskiy, a military correspondent of the Soviet Pravda news agency, wrote of this time:

> All night long in the foggy skies over Budapest would be the hum of German transport aircraft. The powerful searchlight installations would cross their beams, sharp and shining, like dress swords. The automatic anti-aircraft guns and quadruple mounted machine guns sent bursts of tracer bullets and shells up into the sky. Turning over Pest, the Germans flew across the Danube to drop their cargoes of provisions and ammunition to their own soldiers blockaded in Buda. They flew very high for fear of anti-aircraft artillery. The fog made their navigation difficult, and the parachutes [with cargo containers] more often than not fell into the Danube or onto the embankments, and into the streets of Pes, where our soldiers would pick them up.

The Soviets observed some unusual activity by enemy transport aircraft. Lieutenant P.M. Galkin of the 23rd Separate Air Observation, Warning and Communication Stations Battalion recalled:

> The term 'sky' took on a whole new meaning that we had not seen before It was filled with aircraft and spread out over the Buda hills near the settlement of Pilisvorosvar, north-east of Budapest. The sky thundered, and hummed, aircraft were flying in every direction. They were flying in several stages. Highest of all were the He

111s, a little lower were the Ju 52s, lower still – our Il-2 ground-attack aircraft, and almost at ground level were the Po-2 night bombers.

Meantime, the position of the encircled forces continued to deteriorate. On the evening of 17 January, the general in charge of SS land forces in Budapest, Karl Pfeffer-Wildenbruch, received permission to abandon Pest and evacuate the remainder of the garrison to Buda. The German and Hungarian forces had two bridges remaining at their disposal across the Danube: the Elizabeth and the Szechenyi Chain Bridge, which, although they had suffered from air attacks, had survived thanks to constant repairs. Many Hungarian soldiers had deliberately fallen behind their units, with officers and men hiding in basements and refusing to advance any further under such furious Soviet fire and bombardment. Incidents were recorded of the deliberate draining of fuel to immobilize vehicles. Still, several thousand men had gathered on both bridges in the hope of getting across to Buda under heavy artillery fire and bombing by Soviet aircraft. The quartermaster of the 1st Hungarian Armored Tank Division, Lieutenant Colonel A. Vayda, who survived the war, recalled:

> Coarse Hungarian, and German swearwords were flying around all over the place. There was absolute panic, which only grew worse after we had to walk down narrow streets, passing burning buildings. The crowd just took us along with them, and there was no way to escape. An unbearable heat emanated from inside the burning buildings, and a hail of burning window frames and other wooden wreckage fell between the vehicles. Several formations of infantry troops walked on foot between these vehicles. German Feldgendarme [military police] on motorcycles tried to impose at least some semblance of order, but without any real success.
>
> The injured groaned and cried out in pain. By some miracle we managed to get across to the squares on the edge of Pest, next to the Szechenyi Chain suspension bridge. There we were greeted with a scene of absolutely charred ruins. It was the middle of the night and yet it was almost as bright as daylight. Water could be seen through the enormous gaping holes in the bridge. The back end of a German automobile that had unfortunately fallen into one of these holes, stuck up in the air. The forward part, which had gone down deep, was no longer visible. The driver and passengers most likely perished. In another location a truck, that had sustained a direct hit that had only just missed us, was on fire. The bodies of the fallen were lying everywhere. Several people had witnessed vehicles running over them on more than one occasion.

Hungarian historian Y. Ungvari cites the words of an unknown German soldier:

> The infantry abandoned Pest across what was left of the two bridges over the Danube. The soldiers saved their own lives and paid no attention to the bombing. The order to abandon the bridges immediately caused panic. A Police Battalion under General K. Hichler, which had sustained heavy losses prior to their arrival at the strongholds, had lost between 200 and 300 men in the space of a few hours. Some of the Feldgendarmerie detachment, the 13th Panzer Division [and] the Luftwaffe's anti-aircraft crews had been completely wiped out by artillery fire. The bridges were constantly being strafed but the people, who paid no attention to this at all, moved forward. The mixed group of automobiles and trucks, and carts that were covered in tarpaulins, civilian refugees, mothers with crying children, and many, many wounded – they were all in a hurry to get to Buda.

One of the Soviet aviators who distinguished himself during the attack on the bridges across the Danube was a navigator in the 210th Ground Attack Air Regiment (136th Ground Attack Air Division), Hero of the Soviet Union Captain G.F. Sivkov. In making several sorties a day in the short, bright days at the end of December, he hit targets in districts of Pest close to the bridges with bombs and rockets. He also hit the bridges themselves, making three or four bombing runs against each, despite fierce small-caliber anti-aircraft artillery fire. On his 21st combat sortie over Budapest, observers identified 12 direct hits from his Il-2 on the road and supports, principally of the railway bridges, movement over which had been rendered impossible. Grigoriy Flegontovich Sivkov, who was recommended at the end of February 1945 for his second 'Gold Star', had at this time flown 181 successful sorties in his Il-2, plus 42 in an Su-2. By the end of the war, he had completed a total of 246 sorties.

In mid-January, German night ground-attack aircraft and glider pilots had been drafted in to fly into the encircled Hungarian capital, yet those who made such flights without incident, let alone returned to base safely, were few in number. Ober-Gefreiter A. Schlupmann from 2/LLG2 was one of those who were lucky enough to survive the glider flights into Budapest. Later, while in captivity, he stated: "Our group came under the jurisdiction of the 'Konrad' command headquarters and was directly subordinate to the headquarters of the 4th Air Fleet. As they were located on Pápa aerodrome we were tasked with supplying the Budapest [defenders]." His third sortie to Budapest, carrying a cargo of 1,000kg of flour, turned out to be a fateful one – on the night of 20/21 January, after failing to identify the pre-arranged signal on the ground after detaching at an altitude of 2,300m, Schlupmann landed in the eastern part of Pest, and for several days he wandered around this unfamiliar, war-torn city before he gave himself up and became a prisoner of war on 25 January.

Schlupmann had joined the German Army in 1941 and had first served in an aerodrome guard company. In April 1943, he enrolled in the glider pilot's school at Liederbach near Frankfurt am Main, where he studied for four months. Up until April 1944, he for the most part was stationed in Strasbourg as part of the 1st Parachute Assault Squadron LLG1, flying the DFS 230 glider. Following the Allied landings in Normandy in June 1944, they were pulled back to central Germany and were later sent to Vienna, from where they were deployed to the southern Hungarian city of Pecs, having transferred to come under the operational command of NSGr19 under Major E. Janke. The glider pilots began to convert to flying the Ju 87, but this process was never finished and the group again returned to Germany.

According to Schlupmann, 16 pilots and 34 technical staff were redeployed to the Hungarian Pápa aerodrome north-east of the city on 14 January 1945. It was there that many of the transport aircraft were based, as was Generalleutnant Konrad's headquarters. Also on the Pápa aerodrome were 20 gliders and four or five Ju 87s, which had been adapted to operate as tugs. Over the course of 19 and 20 January, Schlupmann observed up to 10 FW 190s taking off from this aerodrome several times, flying to the east and north-east towards Budapest. It was envisaged that the glider pilots, after landing, would be rescued from the pocket and returned to their own lines in an Fi 156 communications aircraft, along with the gliders, which had for the first time actually succeeded in their mission.

The situation for the encircled defenders of Budapest was growing worse by the day. On 29 January, the eve of the anniversary of the Nazis coming to power, special 'celebratory' containers were dropped on the city courtesy of Reichsführer-SS Heinrich Himmler. When they were opened, sweets, cigarettes and jars of horsemeat were found inside, the latter being by then the principal ration for the defenders of Budapest. Hundreds of horses were eaten by the garrison, since there was nothing to feed them on anyway. The following day, an official protest came out of the pocket concerning the contents of Himmler's special containers!

As previously mentioned, the KG4 Squadron had bombed the logistics assets of the 3rd Ukrainian Front several times, but its principal objective remained the transportation of cargoes for the encircled Hungarian troops in Budapest. Soviet reconnaissance confirmed that Germany's main transport aircraft at this time remained the three-engine Ju 52, which had been well-known to Allied forces since 1941. It was these aircraft that were entrusted with the vast majority of the 1,446 flights undertaken to transport cargoes in Hungary in January 1945; the Air Observation, Warning and Communication stations of the 3rd Ukrainian Front recorded 1,149 flights, while the 2nd Ukrainian Front recorded a further 297. Around a quarter of all these flights were carried out with the aim of delivering cargoes to the Hungarian and German garrison. The report of Soviet air observation forces stated: "Enemy transport aviation, flying predominantly Ju 52s both individually and in pairs, by night and by day in inclement weather conditions, delivered cargoes to the encircled troop alignment in Budapest. The cargoes themselves were for the most part dropped onto sites that had been pre-prepared by the troops in the area around Buda."

During the last days of January, the Axis air defenses in the city grew noticeably weaker, having incurred heavy loss, and experienced a shortage of anti-aircraft shells of all calibers, while their fighters only appeared periodically. Consequently, Soviet aircraft losses reduced considerably. Thus, on three occasions on 27 January, Bostons from the 48th Bomber Air Regiment bombed Buda Castle, with an excellent strike rate on the target, for which the regiment's navigator, Captain S.M. Margaryan, received the gratitude of the commander of the 5th Air Army. Regimental documents indicate that the 48th Bomber Air Regiment alone destroyed up to 1,000 buildings in Budapest over the course of the siege (although this claim was a significant exaggeration). The regiment had acted successfully prior to this point, raids involving the regiment's entire complement in January 1945 having led to the destruction of several buildings which were converted into strongholds (this being confirmed by eyewitnesses on the ground).

The weakening of the slender German supply line, which never turned into a steady flow, was a cause for concern for the encircled and now seriously endangered troops, who were concerned that the supplies could dry up completely. One of the most important reasons was the transfer of transport aviation over to assisting their own troops fighting on the outer front. General Balck, who had led the army group that bore his name, reported on 30 January: "With the aim of ensuring the supply of those formations fighting in the area around Esztergom, in case they are cut off by the enemy or caught out by the flood water, sites for dropping cargoes and landing sites for transport gliders, as well as for light 'Storch' aircraft, are to be reconnoitered."

In the opinion of the Soviet Command, the 190th Guards Air Regiment (III Ground Attack Air Corps) led by Lieutenant Colonel I.P. Melnikov was the most efficient fighting unit in the battle for Budapest. Melnikov had fought in the war from the second day (23 June 1941) on the Eastern Front, and he formed the 570th Ground Attack Air Regiment in May 1942. The regiment had been commanded continuously by Melnikov, who had secured the Guards title for the regiment. Melnikov's troops fought with great success in Hungary: it often fought in inclement weather and was particularly successful at striking strongholds. For distinguished fighting in February 1945, the unit was awarded the honorable title of the 'Budapest' Regiment. Soviet documents note: "The combat experience acquired on the front line of the war, and their devotion to their Motherland, their commander's strength of will and their administrative ability assisted Lieutenant Colonel Melnikov in bringing the regiment that he led to a leading position in the division."

The Soviet leadership's perspective on the 2nd Ukrainian Front battles was that regimental crews displayed courage and valor, while the technical personnel showed selfless and tireless work in preparing the aircraft for combat and repairing damage. In flying some 1,607 sorties, the 190th Guards Ground Attack Regiment lost 11 crews, which was the best loss ratio in the III Guards Air Corps, and most likely in the entire 5th Air Army. Prior to the final destruction of the Budapest garrison, the commander of the 12th Guards Ground Attack Air Division, Lieutenant Colonel L.A. Chizhikov, recommended Melnikov for his fourth honorable award – the order of the Red Banner – noting that he had flown 33 mission sorties, including as group leader for three ground-attack sorties against strongholds in the besieged city, and had amassed 153 hours of flying time on the Il-2, while his total number of flying hours stood at 2,235.

January had been a successful month for the III Guards Ground Attack Corps. It had flown 2,885 mission sorties, 2,163 (or 75 percent) of which were aimed at targets in Budapest. Documents testify to its Il-2s carrying an average of 344kg of bombs, not including underslung rocket armament. Up to 30 tanks, 290 vehicles and four tankers were damaged or destroyed by the corps, while 20 field batteries and 18 anti-aircraft batteries were suppressed, and 50 large explosions were caused in the city itself. In battles against German fighters, the corps' crews shot down three FW 190s and one Bf 109. The 279th Fighter Air Division, which had been attached to the corps, recorded a further eight victories. The corps' own combat losses were 17 Il-2s (of which 11 were shot down by anti-aircraft fire), a further nine ground attack aircraft written off as combat losses and a single La-5; 15 ground-attack pilots were either lost or reported missing without trace, as were 16 gunners and one fighter pilot.

Redeployment of a SdKfz10/4 20mm anti-aircraft gun to a new position

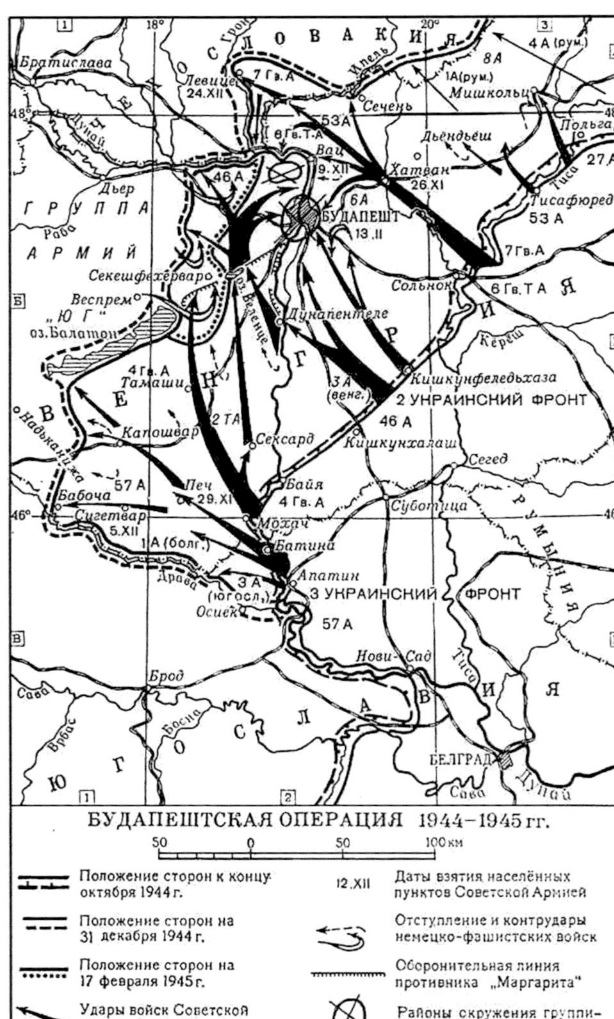

The plan for the Budapest Offensive Operation.

Il-2 of one of the regiments of the 5th Air Army at an airfield in the vicinity of Budapest, 1945.

Il-2 of one of the regiments of the III Guards Attack Air Corps. The aircraft most likely was manufactured before autumn 1943, as the fuselage star does not have the white trim.

Il-2 of the 91st Guards Attack Air Regiment, 4th Guards ShAD, 5th ShAK. Note the removed rear section of the canopy.

Il-2 of one of the regiments of the10th Attack Air Corps, 17th Air Army.

Pe-2 of the 511th Detached Reconnaissance Air Regiment, spring 1945.

Yak-3 of the 'Sword' group, 150th Guards Fighter Air Regiment, 13th Guards IAD. The fighter was flown by Lieutenant S.V. Nosov, who claimed seven air victories over Hungary.

Yak-3 of the 897th IAP, 288th IAD, 17th Air Army, winter–spring 1945.

La-5F of the 177th Guards IAP, 14th Guards IAD, 5th Air Army, 1945. The aircraft was flown by Guards Captain K.S. Maltsev.

Yak-9M of the 513rd IAP, 331st IAD, 5th Air Army

Yak-9U flown by Major A.M. Reshetov of the 31st Guards IAP, 6th Guards IAD, 5th Air Army. This pilot scored his last air victory in the sky over Hungary on 23 March 1945.

Yak-9U of one of the regiments of the 331st IAD, 5th Air Army.

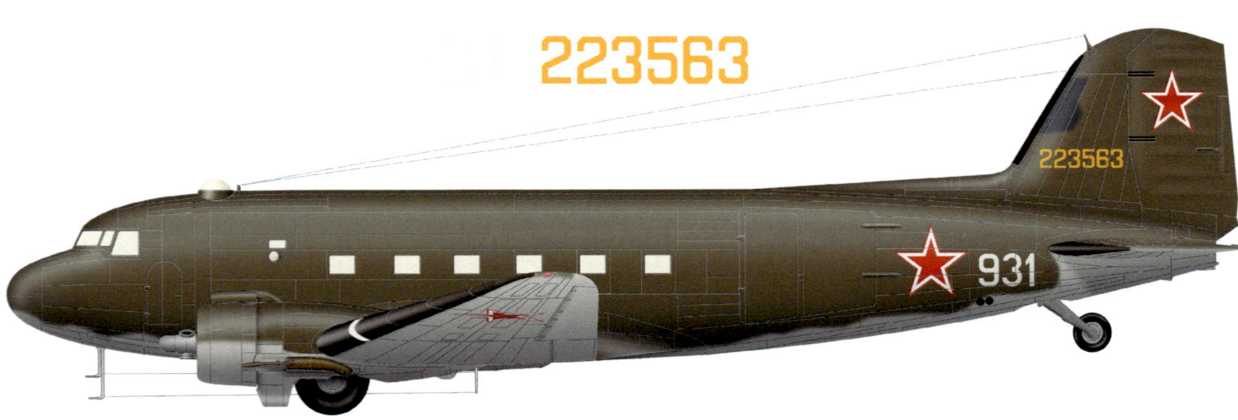

C-47 used for transporting tank engines by one of the transport regiments in Hungary, 1945.

Po-2 of one of the Guards air regiments of the 17th Air Army.

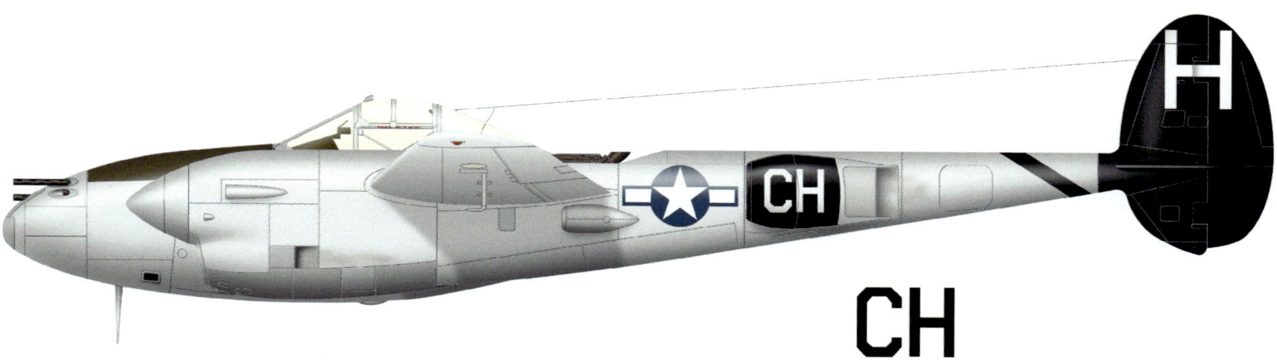

P-38L which belonged to the 95th Fighter Squadron, 82nd Fighter Group. The aircraft was operated in the daytime over Hungary but based at an airfield in Italy.

Bf 109G-10 of the *6/JG52*, Veszprem, Hungary, February 1945.

Bf 109G-14 s/n 611022 of the *102/1 'Ricsi'* which was flown by Captain Laslo Pottyondy, who had 14 air victories by the close of the war.

Bf 109G-14 of the *I/JG53*, Veszprem, Hungary, 4 February 1945. This aircraft was flown by *Hauptmann* Erich Hartmann.

Fw 190F-8 of the *I./SG2*, Hungary, January 1945.

Fw 190F-8 of the *102/1 'Puli'*, January 1945.

He 111H-20s of the *1/KG4* carried out air drops of supply containers to German and Hungarian troops in sieged Budapest.

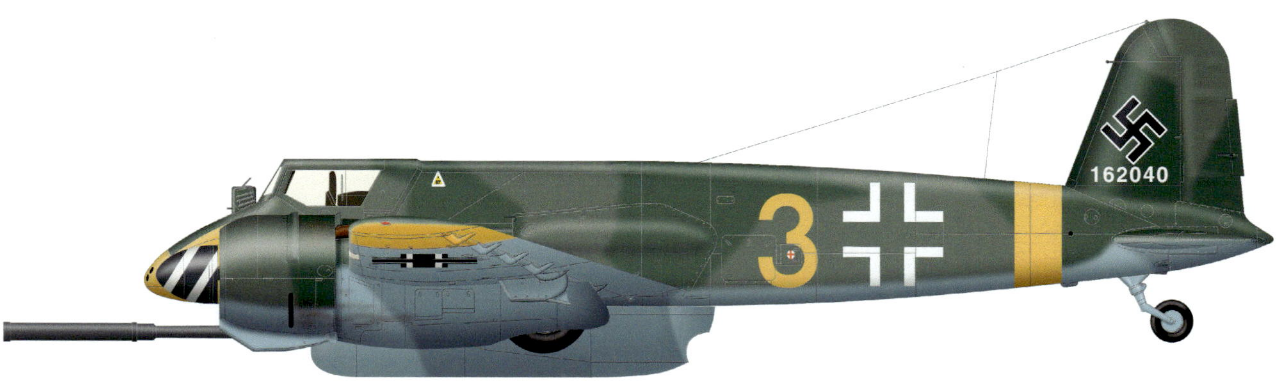

This Hs 129B-3 of the *14(Pz)/SC9* was lost in Hungary on 3 January 1945.

Ju 87G-2 of the *SG2* flown by *Oberst* Hans-Ulrich Rudel on the Eastern Front, December 1944–January 1945.

Me 210Ca-1 of the *2/102 Tygrys,* winter 1945.

reparing an Il-2 for operations in one of the detachments of the 5th Ground Attack Air Regiment under General N.P. Kamanin.

Pilots standing next to Yak-9s of the 194th Fighter Air Division discuss their forthcoming sortie.

Red Army troops firing a Maxim machine gun to counter enemy air attacks in western Budapest during January 1945.

On an airfield near Budapest, a group of ground-attack aircraft are readied for take-off. Evidently they had to take off from an uneven and viscous snow-covered surface.

During the course of the battles over Hungary, Soviet ace N.M. Skomorokhov of the 31st Fighter Air Regiment increased his tally considerably: he shot down three enemy aircraft in November 1944, six in December and a further two at the beginning of January 1945. By the end of the war, he had 46 personal and eight shared victories.

After seeing in the war on the border as a regimental commander, I.D. Podgorny had, in February 1943, already led a fighter air corps which then participated in battles at Kursk, Kirovograd, Korsun-Shevchenkivskiy and for the Dnieper, alongwith other operations. For the heroism and courage shown by its crews, the IV Fighter Air Corps was renamed a Guards Air Corps. The corps' pilots also distinguished themselves over Hungary, while the commander himself, now Major General I.D. Podgorny, personally participated in the air battles, flying 127 sorties (a figure obtained on 15 September 1944).

B.A. Smirnov began his military career in Spain, but after distinguishing himself in the battle for Khalkin-Gol he was awarded the title of Hero of the Soviet Union. By the beginning of the Budapest Operation, Colonel Smirnov was commanding the 288th Fighter Air Division, 17th Air Army. Over the course of the war, Boris Aleksandrovich Smirnov received the thanks of the Supreme Commander-in-Chief 19 times, including for the liberation of Hungary.

Hungarian pilot Senior Lieutenant Gusztav Halmav in his parade uniform. It is known that Halmav participated in battles in his Ca.135 not only against regular forces, but also against partisans.

Colonel General Otto Dessloch – one of the *Luftwaffe*'s highest-ranking leaders. After spending several months in the West as the commander of the 3rd Air Fleet, from 22 September 1944 he returned to the East, being posted to the 4th Air Fleet, facilitating air operations in Hungary and the Balkans.

Ground servicing of a multi-purpose Me 210 aircraft from the ranks of the Hungarian Air Force.

An FW 190F ground-attack aircraft from the SG2 'Immelmann' squadron on Raab aerodrome. Technicians are topping up the aircraft's wheel. The photograph was taken following a heavy fall of snow on the airfield.

The nose section of an A-20G aircraft from the 48th Bomber Air Regiment. From the middle of the war, these aircraft, which had arrived in the USSR in large numbers under the lend-lease program, had undergone a significant adaptation to bring their armament and equipment up to Soviet standards.

One of the UIl-2 (or Il-2 training aircraft) with dual controls in the aft cockpit and drastically reduced armament. This aircraft belonged to the 4th Guards Ground Attack Air Division. In the winter of 1944/45, divisional commander Colonel V.F. Sapyrkin took to the skies in this aircraft on numerous occasions.

Soviet soldiers and officers look over an FW 190F that has been shot down and made an emergency landing in the area around Budapest. The aircraft was probably the victim of Red Army small-caliber anti-aircraft artillery.

Hungarian technicians and pilots on a winter aerodrome.

Fuelling Yak-9 fighters from a combined fuel and oil tanker on one of the aerodromes close to the front line.

Senior Lieutenant G.K. Denisenko of the 235th Ground Attack Air Regiment (V Ground Attack Air Corps) and his gunner Senior Sergeant P.P. Kryuchkov ahead of their departure on a sortie, and after a successful conclusion to a flight. Grigory Denisenko began to participate in battles in October 1943, and by the beginning of 1945 had flown around 150 sorties, inflicting an enormous amount of damage on the enemy, for which in 1946 he was awarded the title of Hero of the Soviet Union. The Red Army Air Force also wanted to bestow an accolade on the aircraft's gunner, Panteley Kryuchkov, who had flown 205 sorties by the end of the war, but for some unknown reason he was not awarded the 'Gold Star'.

A repair brigade at work in the 13th Guards Fighter Air Division. The engine cowlings that have been removed from the Yak-1 fighter are visible.

Soviet soldiers in a Ford car pass a German Panzer Mark IV tank that was taken out of action by aerial anti-tank bombs dropped by ground-attack aircraft.

One of the most successful Soviet aces, N.F. Krasnov. After he had graduated from pilot school, he worked as a pilot in the civilian air fleet, from 1938 onwards as a test pilot at OKB-19 and the I.V. Stalin factory No. 19 in Zaporozhye, and from 1941 he fought on the front line of the war against Germany. He was killed in a flying accident near Budapest on 29 January 1945 during his 279th sortie.

The commander of the 3rd Ukrainian Front, Marshal F.I. Tolbukhin, in his operations cabin in Hungary.

Regent Miklos Horthy de Nagybanya's palace, also known as Buda castle, was captured in a Red Army assault following powerful strafing and bombing attacks.

The crew (both air and ground crew) standing next to an A-20G aircraft of the Soviet 860th Bomber Air Regiment (17th Air Army). On the right is squadron commander Captain V.V. Roginets, who distinguished himself in the Budapest Operation during an attack on Harkány station.

Teleki Street in Budapest, following a raid by aircraft of the 305th Ground Attack Air Division (10th Ground Attack Air Corps) on defensive positions.

A German Ju 52 transport aircraft which was involved in an accident during an emergency landing in the snow, during an attempt to get through to the encircled garrison in the Hungarian capital.

A German armored personnel carrier destroyed following strafing and bombing near a fence around a Budapest park.

7

January 1945

According to Soviet records, its pilots were involved in many successful dogfights, one of the most successful of which took place on 3 January. On that day, a group of six aircraft from the 178th Fighter Air Regiment (led by Senior Lieutenant P.R. Shchetinin) provided cover for ground troops north-west of Budapest. After receiving a message from a guidance station about the approach of German Messerschmitts (belonging to I/JG53 and II/JG51), Shchetinin warned his pilots over the radio, which enabled them to beat off the first attack – which had come out of the sun – without loss. At that time, a further eight Bf 109s arrived, but thanks to the spirit among the crews and the actions of the aircraft flown by Captain V.A. Semyonov and Senior Lieutenant P.A. Bryzgalov, the enemy were again unable to achieve any successes. A III Guards Fighter Air Corps' report on the incident observed:

> As a result of decisive, and bold attacks by our fighters, the enemy formation was destroyed, [and] the Messerschmitts were forced to fight in pairs. Since they had a numerical advantage not only did the enemy beat off our attacks but they actively counter-attacked as well. During the course of the battle the ground-attack and maneuvering [Soviet] pairs of aircraft cooperated successfully, assisting one another. The escorting pair led by Senior Lieutenant Bryzgalov kept a sharp lookout ... After losing six of their aircraft in a 20-minute battle, the enemy was forced to abandon the fight. Our group did not incur any losses.

An Il-2 ground-attack aircraft from the 5th Air Army of General S.K. Goryunov over the central district of Buda.

Street battles for the city. Artillery and aviation strikes have cleared the streets for Soviet attack groups.

Squadron commander of the 122nd Fighter Air Regiment (331st Fighter Air Division) Captain V.V. Rybalka standing next to a Yak-9. He started the war as a sergeant based just outside Moscow, but finished the war in Vienna, having flown more than 300 sorties. After the war, Vitaliy Viktorovich Rybalka was made commander of the 73rd Air Army.

One of the streets of Budapest during the operation. Soviet anti-aircraft artillery served a dual purpose here: for defense against air attacks and firing at enemy land-based hardware and barricades.

A Ju 52 transport from TG1 is readied for a sortie to deliver cargoes to the encircled German and Hungarian garrison in Budapest. Soon after the start of the battle for the city, it became impossible to land transport aircraft within the encirclement owing to round-the-clock Soviet fire and the bombing of aerodromes and landing strips.

An He 111 aircraft from KG4 that has been damaged by anti-aircraft artillery. Evidently the aircraft has been painted in a matt paint for night-time operations.

German and Hungarian glider pilots standing next to their Go 242 glider on a snowy aerodrome not far from Lake Balaton.

Supply containers, dropped from German aircraft in the area around Krovaviy Lug, fall to earth by parachute.

Soviet anti-aircraft artillery preparing to fire on aircraft and gliders in Buda.

Preparing a Messerschmitt from I/JG53 for a sortie.

A Soviet 1939 model 88mm 52-K anti-aircraft gun and its crew fire on enemy aircraft.

The area around Krovaviy Lug and the containers that were dropped here.

Soviet anti-aircraft crews in a ground battle in the city.

An Il-2 on the attack.

This German Hummel self-propelled gun has been put out of action next to the walls of a house.

One of the 210th Ground Attack Air Regiment's documents records not only the courage and heroism of G.F. Sivkov, who was subsequently twice made a Hero of the Soviet Union, but also his capabilities in accurate air navigation skills in difficult circumstances and his ability to master skills from the young, competent and brave ground-attack pilots subordinated to him.

German technicians carry underslung tanks for fighter aircraft. With their help the flight range for the Bf 109G increased considerably, enabling them to escort aircraft like the He 111 on their flights into the Budapest 'pocket'.

The 90th Guards Ground Attack Air Regiment on Ternava airfield. In the foreground is an Il-2 aircraft, while to the right with a map-board is the unit's commander, Lieutenant Colonel M.A. Ischenko.

The Hungarian parliament buildings in January 1945. They were constructed at the beginning of the 20th century and were the largest building complex in Budapest.

A view of Krovaviy Lug following the surrender of the remaining German and Hungarian forces in Budapest.

This recently manufactured but dismantled Bf 109K fighter belonging to JG53 was abandoned during the German withdrawal in early of 1945.

A German He 111H bomber of *KG4* attempting to take off from a snowy aerodrome to drop supplies to the encircled garrison in the Hungarian capital, in early January 1945.

A delegation of cavalrymen of the IV Cossack Cavalry Corps are guests of the pilots of the 10thGround Attack Air Corps (17th Air Army) in January 1945. Fourth from the right is the commander of the 31st Fighter Air Regiment, Hero of the Soviet Union Lieutenant Colonel G.D. Onufrienko; sixth from the right is the regiment's most successful ace, Captain N.M. Skomorokhov, who was to become twice Hero of the Soviet Union.

Standing on an aerodrome is an unserviceable Hs 129B aircraft that has been captured by Soviet troops during the winter of 1944/45.

An 88mm anti-aircraft gun destroyed in an air raid by ILs at one of the strongholds of German and Hungarian forces in Pest.
23v. Fighter pilot I.S. Prozor of the 85th Guards Fighter Air Regiment stands next to his Yak-1 during the spring of 1945.

8

Budapest, February 1945

In early February, 5th Air Army's Command and headquarters, in their execution of a Directive issued by the commander of the 2nd Ukrainian Front, Marshal R.Y. Malinovsky, devised an aviation battle plan aimed at concluding the Budapest Operation. The document envisaged the liquidation of the encircled forces by means of bombers and ground-attack aircraft, together with ground troops, in the shortest possible time. The Red Army Air Force fighter regiments were to destroy the enemy's transport aircraft that were bringing in ammunition, supplies and hardware to Budapest, and provide cover for the districts containing Soviet concentrations of troops to protect them from attacks by enemy aircraft.

Meantime, flights by German transport aircraft to the pocket continued. Occasionally, even transport gliders would be sent to Budapest. A small airstrip was used for them to land on in the western part of the city, known as Krovaviy Lug. Owing to the proximity of multi-storey buildings nearby, however, landing there was considered highly dangerous: on 4 February, a DFS-230 flown by Feldwebel G. Filius flew into a seven-storey building while trying to land. The glider's crumpled framework and its damaged cargo were left sticking out of the building following his accident, ensuring that Krovaviy Lug proved worthy of its name.[1] In total, I./LLG2 sent 48 gliders into Budapest (a report by German Transport Command revealed total losses among gliders were 73 DFS 230s).

Contemporary German chronicles record that the final flights to in 'fortress' Budapest were made on 12 February, and the garrison surrendered the following day. In total, over six months, Axis aircraft and gliders had delivered approximately 1,500 tons of cargo into the besieged city, for which the Luftwaffe's transport section lost 44 aircraft – 36 Ju 52s, seven He 111s and one Ju 87. Hungarian historian P. Posztoni cites even greater losses:

> The significant losses that were the cost of this operation, do not correspond at all with its results: the 'air bridges' from Pápa–Budapest, or from Szombathely–Budapest cost 105 aircraft, and 138 men [aircrew] killed, injured or missing without trace. In the end Lieutenant General G. Konrad, who had led the supply service for the besieged city of Budapest, was forced to admit that he had not been able to fulfill the task that he had been given. Owing to the constant reinforcement of the Russian anti-aircraft defense, supplying the troops using the 'air bridges' had to be stopped. The last aircraft to carry a cargo was shot down on 9 February 1945 directly over the Royal Palace in Pest.

From around 20 January, the situation for the encircled troops and formations was hopeless. The Axis forces, however, stubbornly refused to acknowledge this and surrender. Far from all the Hungarian and German forces abandoned Pest on 17 and 18 January, even though the majority of the city was by then in the hands of Soviet troops, while in Buda, the Germans and troops loyal to Ferenc Szálasi decided to fight to the last man. The majority of their anti-aircraft artillery batteries had concentrated there, but the reserve of shells was considerably reduced, so Soviet aircraft losses did not increase. A protracted absence of Soviet reinforcements in terms of aircraft could not fail to have a negative effect on the combat capability of the ground-attack formations. First and foremost, this relates to those that participated directly in beating back the attacks on the besiegers' outer front. There were days when no more than 20 Soviet ground-attack aircraft would get airborne. The technicians, mechanics and other aviation specialists restored these aircraft, and repaired the damaged Ils round-the-clock, eating and sleeping on the aerodromes.

The commander of the V Ground Attack Air Corps, General N.P. Kamanin, wrote of the current state of play in his diary at the end of January: "The battle for Buda continues. We are flying between 100 and 120 sorties per day with ground-attack aircraft, and between 50 and 60 sorties per day with fighters. There are no enemy fighters over Buda. The anti-aircraft fire is weak. The pilots make between eight and 10 approaches each to the target, returning without incurring losses."

An officer of the Soviet XXIII Rifle Corps observed the enemy and their manners closely at the close of the siege:

> On the night of 12 February the Hitlerites made a desperate attempt at breaking through into the XXXVII Rifle Corps' sector. They obstinately

1 The Russian name *Krovaviy Lug* translates as 'Bloody Meadow'.

> continued to break away to the west and north-west towards Zugliget and Nadkovachi on the bodies of their fallen officers and men. In the end 16,000 [in reality this was more like 12,000] fascists succeeded in breaking through the encirclement and hiding in the nearby forests.

Next morning, the Soviets organized a search of this forest area.

Although the surrounding Soviet forces could not prevent this large body of Axis troops from breaking out, the majority of them met a tragic fate. As of 11 February, around 44,000 officers and men remained under Pfeffer-Wildenbruch in and around Budapest. By 15 February, approximately 17,000 of them had been killed and some 22,350 captured. For the most part, they fell or were taken prisoner in the first six hours of their bid for escape between Széll Kálmán Square and Hűvösvölgy. Around 3,000 men were able to hide in the mountains, but by 17 February the majority of them had given themselves up. Only 785 officers and men eventually reached the German lines, while around 700 hid within Budapest itself.

Following this, a truly apocalyptic scene was playing out in Budapest, with mountains of bodies, human remains that had been crushed by tank tracks and torn to pieces by explosions from aerial bombs, and bridges spattered with blood and body parts. On Széll Kálmán Square and at Vérhalom and in other nearby locations, the bodies were piled up to a height of several meters. They were committed to the earth in several cemeteries – within the Hungarian capital alone there were 28 mass burial sites, while in the suburbs, where around 5,000 bodies were found, there were even more such sites. As a result of the storming of the city, many of the civilian population also perished; they were interned along with the officers and men.

It is likely that 5th Air Army made the biggest contribution to the execution of the air blockade of Budapest. The commander of the Budapest Group, Lieutenant General I.M. Managarov, gave the actions of the III Guards Ground Attack Air Corps an exceptionally high rating:

> The corps' commander and the divisional commanders were permanently at the rifle corps and divisional observation posts. After distinctly organizing their own units, they responded immediately to the issues raised by ground forces. The personnel in the individual units demonstrated a high degree of skill, as well as bravery and courage in their execution of their orders. The pilots flew between five and six sorties and were a constant presence in the air over the enemy, making it harder for them to offer any resistance to the advancing forces. As soon as the ground-attack aircraft had been alerted they would always arrive at exactly the right time and would not leave the battlefield until they had used up all their ammunition. In spite of the difficulties of orientating around the city and the poor visibility, the corps did not suffer from friendly fire. The author is of the opinion that the III Guards Ground Attack Air Corps coped very well with the tasks put before them to destroy the besieged enemy.

The commission's, which was founded by 17th Air Army headquarters, work is recorded in surviving memoirs. Its aim was to ascertain the effectiveness of bombing and ground-attack strikes on the city and its besieged garrison. The group of squadron navigator Captain G.P. Yevdokimov from the 449th Bomber Air Regiment started its inspection in Pest, and Grigoriy Petrovich Yevdokimov recalled:

> The trail of destruction and hunger was visible all over the city. The streets were half deserted; on the rare occasion that we did see someone walking through the city in civilian clothes they were emaciated, and indifferent to anything that was happening. The skeletons of horses, dogs and cats were lying on the bridges. Gliders were stranded on the roofs and cornices of several buildings, along with the offcuts of cargo parachutes. We had to bed down for the night in the barracks once occupied by a military unit.
>
> The next morning we went to Buda. As it turned out all the bridges across the Danube had been demolished by the retreating German forces, and moreover they had been demolished just as a lively flow of buses, trams and pedestrians were crossing them. Hundreds of innocent people including women and children perished in the waters of the Danube. The owner of a private boat rowed us over to Buda, which had become the last stronghold of the encircled garrison, for half a crust of bread. In contrast to Pest this part of the city had sustained very heavy damage. For three days we crept around the craters caused by the explosions of aerial bombs, taking in the broken and damaged facilities. In the process of doing this work our soldiers were constantly driving the captured German soldiers and officers out of the fortress. These dirty-looking men, who had not shaved for a considerable time, were shabby, dressed each in their own fashion, and had haunting, fearful glances on their faces – they had witnessed something unpleasant that had caused them revulsion.

This commission, which had been organised by order of Lieutenant General O.V. Tolstikov, had a more distinct mission to fulfill: study of air strike results by 10thGround Attack Air Corps on bridges across the Danube in Budapest. In total, 38 sorties had been flown using 227 Ils against the four bridges, which varied in width from 12–26m and supported the movement of road and tram traffic. The commission for the most part put the attacks' relatively low effectiveness down to the inability of the bombs to strike the load-bearing sections of the target, since FAB-100 and FAB-250 bombs were used with a delayed explosive fuse. In order to achieve the required result, larger bombs with a caliber of 500–1,000kg would have been required.

In accordance with their mission statement, the Soviet ground-attack aircraft were to approach the target in level flight at an altitude of 800–1,100m and drop their bombs from heights of between 500m and 300m. However, since more often than not at the time there was poor visibility over the city, with lingering fog, the attacks on the Budapest bridges were carried out from an altitude of not more than 100m, and the pilots approached their target at an angle of 15–20°. It turned out that 49 FAB-100 and 13 FAB-250 bombs had hit the bridge supports and roadways, but around half of the ordnance had ricocheted off the targets and many of the others had fallen into the river, yet not before they had broken through the outer layer of the road bridge (they were fitted with delayed timers). The commission concluded that four bridges had been damaged, but not one of them had collapsed; the ground-attack corps had needed 15 sorties for each incident of damage caused to a bridge, which was approximately six times less than during the bombing of the River Dniepr at Dnipropetrovsk and Kremenchuk in the autumn of 1943.

By early February, the scale of destruction in the Hungarian capital was massive, and the defenders were often at a loss to explain just what had happened: had a wall collapsed as a result of a direct hit from a heavy shell or the blast from an aerial bomb? There was not one building left intact on Rokus-hegy. Boszormenyi street, at Budapest's South station, Széll Kálmán Square or on Margit Boulevard – all had been turned into ruin. In the area around the castle, one could only guess at where the streets had once stood as everything lay in a heap of bricks, bits of wood and cement dust. Often the inhabitants preferred to move around the city on the roofs of the ruined buildings. Sh. Marai, a resident of Budapest, described this scene as follows:

> What I witnessed in the area around Óbuda Island looked awful at first glance ... It gave the impression that my route did not pass through the districts of a city, but across archaeological excavations. One could only guess that some of the streets had even existed at all: here was a corner house, there was the 'Florian' café, and here was the street where I had once lived. Not one building [was] left intact. Just heaps of junk on the corner of Statistical Street and Margit Boulevard, there were just a few days ago a five-storey apartment block and café had once towered ... Trams wrecked by direct hits from bombs and rockets on Krovaviy Lug, in Krisztinaváros district, near Nap-hegy and in the environs of the Castle added to the picture of complete desolation."

Despite the vast devastation, Budapest had suffered much less than Warsaw following the German suppression of the uprising of autumn 1944, or had Stalingrad, where in the course of a massive bombardment on the evening of 23 August 1942 alone more than 40,000 inhabitants had been killed. It is now known that the Red Army Air Force, despite orders from Stalin, had barely used FAB-500 bombs or larger munitions in the support of ground troops in the street battles. In Budapest, which before the war had been considered one of the most beautiful cities in Europe, only some 4.6 percent of all housing had been destroyed completely, while another 6.4 percent were damaged but repairable. By way of comparison, in Warsaw some 75 percent of houses were destroyed, including 90 percent of the historical monuments, while Stalingrad lost 85 percent of its housing; in Voronezh the figure had been 97 percent, and almost no residential buildings were left standing after the siege of Sevastopol in the Crimea.

As the destruction of the trapped German and Hungarian forces had been going on, localized battles continued on the encirclement's outer front. German aircraft activity was not excessive. German sources note that the most visible aircraft were FW 190s; the SG10 squadron was active, as well as 1/SG2 group, which had remained at Győr aerodrome (which the Germans named Raab) following the redeployment of other formations from the 2nd Ground Attack Squadron back to Germany. The small losses that they did incur were linked to accurate ground fire, as evidenced by the commander of 2/SG10, Ober-Leutnant Hans Schulz, who undcer interrogation provide full and exhaustive information to the counterintelligence department of the Soviet 17th Air Army headquarters.

Schulz was a very experienced pilot who had completed 486 sorties, during which in addition to attacking ground targets he had shot down seven Soviet aircraft, including three over Hungarian territory. He revealed that the principal tactic for the German ground-attack crews in the winter of 1944-45 was to fly sorties in pairs and groups of four and then engage in 'free hunting' for columns of vehicles, railway traffic close behind Soviet lines and troop concentrations. A recommendation that he receive a Knight's Cross was never followed through. On 10 February 1945, a 37mm anti-aircraft shell hit the engine of his Focke-Wulf, forcing him to make an emergency landing behind Soviet lines. Schulz said he was certain that all seven FW 190Fs lost in his group (comprising some 20 aircraft) from the beginning of 1944 onwards behind the front line, which amounted to the squadron's entire losses over that period, succumbed to ground fire.

Having reduced the large enemy forces around Budapest, the Soviet Command were optimistic that they could build on their success. On 17 February, General Headquarters sent two directives to the commanders of the 2nd and 3rd Ukrainian Fronts, Marshals Malinovsky and Tolbukhin. The first required them to prepare, and to begin by 15 March, an offensive towards Bratislava, Brno and Vienna, with the objective of capturing the Austrian capital within 20 days. The second directive ordered the regrouping of the forces of the two fronts, and their augmentation with the fresh 9th Guards Army from the Headquarters reserve.

The German armed forces paid a great deal of attention to ensuring the element of surprise in their subsequent operations. Not only did they change the names of all combat formations arriving in the region from the Ardennes in their radio traffic, as well as on service documentation and maps, to, for example, 'training', 'columns of construction equipment' or 'reserve groups'; they took the service record books from the panzer forces personnel, removed their brassards, and changed the field post-office numbers. The impression was created on the front line of the organization of a strong, long-lasting defense, and the Germans spread rumors around the local population that the most combat-capable troops were about to be redeployed north to just outside Berlin. Within a few days, at dawn and again in the evening, the withdrawal from the front line of military hardware, trucks and specialist vehicles was simulated, and they would then return via different routes and concentrate close to Székesfehérvár. The aircraft parking areas on their home bases were also carefully disguised. All this assisted the Germans in spreading disinformation to put Soviet intelligence off the scent.

Without waiting for the approach and concentration of all their ground forces, the Germans then attacked the Soviet 7th Guards Army on 17 February from the area around Komarno. As the ensuing week-long battle went on, the Soviets established that the enemy's main attacking force was the I SS Panzer Corps, fighting under *Ober-Gruppenfuhrer-SS* J. Dietrich's Sixth Panzer Army. Despite achieving some success, the Germans had lost the vital element of surprise. In the Soviet headquarters, the conclusion was reached that the advent of a powerful German army presaged the preparation of a large-scale offensive towards Budapest. Prior to this, as discussed above, Soviet commanders had been focused on bringing to fruition their orders for the next offensive against the Germans and their final routing.

"As they were preparing for the offensive, 3rd Ukrainian Front Command kept a watchful eye on the enemy," recalled front-line Chief of Staff General S.P. Ivanov. From mid-February, Soviet reconnaissance forces had begun to provide information on the concentration of a large-scale enemy tank formation in the area around Lake Balaton. Subsequent reports to General Headquarters were initially not believed. The Chief of General Staff General A.I. Antonov, when speaking with 3rd Ukrainian Front commander Marshal Tolbukhin, asked in disbelief: "Who is going to believe you, that Hitler has withdrawn his Sixth SS Panzer Army from the west and has sent them to attack the 3rd Ukrainian Front, and not to an area close to Berlin, where preparations are underway for the final operation to rout German forces?!"

Moscow was initially unconvinced. It was hard for both the Soviet Headquarters and General Headquarters to believe that the German Command would, when Soviet forces were only 60km away from the capital of the Reich, begin to redeploy their best and most combat-capable panzer formations to Hungary and organize a counterattack there. The reliability of the intelligence presented to them, however, was finally confirmed a few days later: a major German force was indeed being concentrated against the 3rd Ukrainian Front, requiring swift responsive measures.

After evaluating the situation, and predicting the direction of the main attack, Marshal Tolbukhin warned the army commanders in chief of the looming German offensive. It was decided that the principal Soviet forces would concentrate to the south and north of Lake Velentse, to create a strong, in-depth anti-tank defense as far as Lake Balaton. Counting on the terrain having been prepared from an engineering perspective, with towns and villages turned into strongholds and a system of obstacles put in place, the German attack would be wiped out using artillery fire and tactical counter-attacks. This was to be achieved without allowing the enemy to break through the front line to any depth, thus creating the conditions for the switch to a wider counter-attack. Soviet defensive forces were built up along an 85km front in two echelons, with a powerful reserve available.

There was an urgent need to restore the strength of Soviet aviation forces in Hungary. More and more modern batches of the most up-to-date aircraft were sent to augment Soviet aviation units with new matériel. It turned out that all, or almost all, of these aircraft had been concentrated in eastern Romania at the beginning of 1945, but due to unfavorable weather conditions they could not be ferried to the aerodromes in Hungary by air. It was then that the Air Army Command took the decision to undertake any further deployment by rail. The 17th Air Army Deputy Chief Engineer, Colonel-Engineer V.I. Frolov, who led a group of technical personnel, coped admirably with the task he was set: eight trains carrying Yak-3 and La-7 aircraft arrived at their new aerodromes by the start of the defensive battle, and these fighters were assembled and flight-tested.

The commander of the neighboring 5th Air Army, General N.P. Kamanin, recalled similar processes in his forces. In the battles for Budapest, his corps lost 26 pilots, including Hero of the Soviet Union Major I.L. Mogilchak of the 235th Ground Attack Air Regiment (who died from burns, having flown 140 missions), as well as 31 air gunners, and was in need of rest and augmentation. The leaders of the V Ground Attack Air Corps participated in an important conference at the end of February to draw interim conclusions under the chairmanship of the Deputy Commander of the Red Army Air Force, Marshal G.A. Vorozheykin, who had coordinated Soviet aviation operations in Hungary. After noting that he had offered a whole host of complimentary words to the aircrew in his corps, Kamanin concluded: "For the last two weeks on the front line nothing of any significance has happened. The aerodromes are now soggy, and our flying is restricted. We continue to augment our regiments with new aircraft and pilots. The snow on the fields has already melted, and the aerodromes are drying out, though slowly."

A Po-2 communication aircraft flying into an airstrip on the right bank of the Danube.

A view of Budapest's factory district taken from a Po-2 aircraft in early February 1945.

A glider carrying a cargo that crashed into a house on Attila Street in Budapest.

An La-5 fitted with AO-25 bombs. Fighters carrying ordnance such as this were used by the 331st Fighter Air Division during the liquidation of the encircled Axis forces.

Soviet troops move around the liberated areas of the city. On the right is a Soviet 61-K 1939 model 37mm automatic anti-aircraft gun.

German hardware on the streets and squares of Budapest that has been hit by enemy fire.

Two ground-attack aircraft pilots clarify their forthcoming sortie on a map.

The commander of the V Ground Attack Air Corps, Major General N.P. Kamanin, who was one of the first to be awarded the title of the Hero of the Soviet Union.

A soldier serving in the aerodrome company cleans the runway ahead of an Me 210 taking off. An SC 50 type bomb carried under the wing is visible.

Two German anti-aircraft guns – 88mm and 37mm – that were destroyed by Soviet air attacks during the blockade.

A Bf 109G from JG53 takes off.

Soldiers from the composite Budapest Group under General I.M. Managarov sitting on the tail of a downed Messerschmitt in the winter of 1945.

A Bf 109G-10 from 6/JG51 under Leutnant Kuhlein takes off in the snow with 300-litre fuel tanks suspended underneath.

This DFS 230 glider with a cargo of flour crashed into a house whilst attempting a landing at Krovaviy Lug. The pilot, Feldwebel Georg Filius, was killed.

A view of a ruined hangar on Budaörs aerodrome, after occupation by Soviet troops, on 15 February 1945.

Among the Soviet trophies was this 88mm anti-aircraft gun mounted on a railway platform.

Marshal R.Y. Malinovsky receives a report in the center of Buda.

The peaceful population of Budapest return to their homes after the conclusion of the battles.

The red flag is raised over the center of Budapest.

One of the city's districts that was destroyed during the course of the 100 days of stubborn fighting.

A view of Pest from a Soviet Yak reconnaissance aircraft. This photograph was taken in February 1945.

The aircrew of the 451st Ground Attack Air Regiment (V Ground Attack Air Corps, 5th Air Army). Second on the right is the unit commander, Lieutenant Colonel N.M. Kosevich.

Personnelof the 511th Separate Reconnaissance Air Regiment standing next to a Pe-2 aircraft. In the center in parade uniform is the unit commander, Lieutenant Colonel S.D. Berman. This photograph was taken after the surrender of the Budapest garrison

Ground-attack pilot Andrey Zvantsov departs on a sortie from an aerodrome near Székesfehérvár of the 17th Air Army in February 1945.

Senior Lieutenant I.M. Sovit (in the centre) of the 31st Guards Fighter Air Regiment (6th Guards Fighter Air Division, III Guards Fighter Air Corps) stands next to his Yak-9, which has a lion emblem on the engine.

9

Failure of the Wehrmacht's Last Offensive

The capture of Budapest on 13 February and the surrender of the remainder of the encircled German and Hungarian forces dramatically changed the balance of power in the south-eastern sector of the Soviet–German front. Hitler was also forced to redeploy his reserves to defend Berlin, fearing the loss of his capital. In this context, the German decision to forestall the invasion of Austria by Soviet forces with a large-scale offensive towards Budapest appeared to be a logical one.

The loss of Austria, western Hungary, and central Czechoslovakia – the heart of the Reich's military-economic base – would massively impact Germany's capability to continue the war. The German High Command, which boosted its counter-attack in Hungary with strategic reserves from the Western Front, began planning Operation *Spring Awakening* soon after the fall of Budapest. *Wehrmacht* records state: "The *Führer*'s decision to deploy the Sixth Panzer Army to Hungary to protect the oil region, which had a decisive effect on the outcome of the war, also suggested that in March along with the forces that had been freed up from this sector, there would be an attack on the central sector of the Eastern Front."

The Germans ran into considerable difficulties in their redeployment of the Sixth Panzer Army, as systematic Soviet air raids on transport hubs had reduced capacity as much as five-fold. Germany no longer had enough coal for its steam locomotives, which would only be distributed by way of a personal order from Hitler. He also ordered the organization of protection for trains, using powerful air defence assets. Despite these problems a reinforced and well-equipped motorized formation had arrived in Hungary, which comprised combat-capable troops who had undergone training in night operations and the most modern hardware. The deployment of special infrared sights for tanks and a large number of armored personnel carriers is particularly worthy of note, the latter enhancing the mobility of German infantry considerably.

The Germans were able to create a specific advantage in terms of tanks and infantry. The Soviet 17th Air Army, however, had more than 1,000 aircraft to oppose them. According to Soviet reconnaissance, the *Luftwaffe* had 850 combat aircraft at their disposal. German reports claimed they had up to 550 German and Hungarian aircraft in the 4th Air Army under Colonel-General O. Dressloch, taking into account the disbandment of the Transport Command and not counting the aircraft owned by the Croatian Air Command. The principal forces, as before, came under the I Air Corps led by General of Aviation D. Deichmann. In order to reduce the reliance on aviation units, the Germans concentrated the most combat-capable fighter units, as well as their ground-attack, short-range reconnaissance, and anti-tank aircraft, on Veszprem north aerodrome, from where they could more easily support their ground forces. (Incidentally, Veszprem was the location of one of the largest cemeteries for *Luftwaffe* personnel, and was where the fallen from a series of Anglo-American raids in the summer of 1944 were laid to rest). The Germans placed their hopes on this new operation taking the Red Army by surprise.

Spring Awakening began on the night of 5/6 March on the southern sector of the 3rd Ukrainian Front. German forces made two attacks in this location: one against units of the 1st Bulgarian and 3rd Yugoslan Armies, preliminarily fording the River Drava, and another against the 57th Soviet Army. Both operations were auxiliary and divergent in nature, as the Germans launched their principal assault on the morning of 6 March between Lakes Velentse and Balaton against the forces of the 26th Army, commanded by Lieutenant General N.A. Gagen. The situation in the skies over Hungary during the course of *Spring Awakening* was in stark contrast to that observed between December 1944 and January 1945, as became clear from the first few hours of the offensive.

Soviet operations reports make it evident that over the course of 6 March, front-line aviation forces flew 358 sorties, shooting down only a single German aircraft in air combat (anti-aircraft crews claimed they had destroyed a second aircraft). The German fliers, according to information from the Soviet Air Observation, Warning and Communication stations, responded with just 87 sorties, although one enormous bombing and strafing attack was observed involving 35 aircraft against our Soviet cdefences near the settlement of János. The relatively low level of aerial activity was partially explained by the weather: dank, low cloud with some breaks, and temperatures barely climbing above freezing, which was not conducive to flying. By way of a comparison, across the entire Soviet–German front, the Red Army Air Force made 3,094 sorties, while the *Luftwaffe* flew 672. The Soviets recorded 29 enemy aircraft being shot down by all methods, including nine on the 2nd Baltic Front (in places, the most high-pressure battles on that day were those at Skrunda,

Kuldīga and Saldus in Latvia), and a further seven shot down on the 1st Belorussian Front.

The Germans unleashed thousands of shells, mines and aerial bombs on Soviet positions, but the defenders steadfastly beat back the attacks, and the offensive made insignificant gains. Accurate fire by Soviet artillery, as well as constant air attacks, inflicted considerable damage on the German forces and slowed the tempo of their advance. The crews of the 17th Air Army fought in close cooperation with the Soviet infantry, with some 227 sorties flown against the Sixth Panzer Army. Attacks on smaller formations by Il-2 ground-attack aircraft using anti-tank bombs were especially effective.

From the early morning, Soviet ground-attack aircraft, and bombers, escorted by fighters, had been taking to the skies. Crews of the 244th Bomber Air Division, using all three of their groups of between 15 and 18 Bostons, attacked columns of Axis tanks and crossing points, also conducting reconnaissance. The Soviet fliers incurred most of their losses at this time from anti-aircraft artillery. As he was flying away from one target, a shell hit Lieutenant Korotkov's bomber from the 449th Bomber Air Regiment, and he departed safely northwards on just one engine. His regimental colleagues of Lieutenant N.I. Vasilyev's crew were not so fortunate: the port side of their Boston's stabilizer flew off and the duralumin over the whole of the tailfin was torn, after which the aircraft went into a spin and crashed to the ground. Other Soviet aviators saw just one parachute open, and it later emerged that the pilot, Vasilyev, and navigator Lieutenant V.P. Lyutiy had both been killed.

Lieutenant Tselapov's aircraft from the 260th Bomber Air Regiment had its oil system destroyed by a direct hit from a shell into the port side; the oil tank was punctured and the air gunner was injured. The pilot restarted the damaged engine and brought his aircraft back to base, where he landed and it was sent for repair. Another incident occurred involving the 260th Bomber Air Regiment when Junior Lieutenant Kolomenchuk was unable to lift his bomber off the ground on take-off and it fell onto its nose; fortunately, it did not catch fire, although it was beyond repair. Fourteen other aircraft in the 244th Division sustained between six and 14 holes from shrapnel, with technical staff working to repair and bring them back into use. As a result of their efforts, the division flew 71 sorties the following day, six more than it had done on 6 March.

Two pilots from the 31st Fighter Air Regiment, Captain N.M. Skomorokhov and Senior Lieutenant V.V. Kirilyuk, were awarded the titles of Heroes of the Soviet Union. At the beginning of March, despite unfavorable weather (rain and fog), they flew together several times on reconnaissance missions to Székesfehérvár, observing large concentrations of enemy tanks. Nikolai Mikahylovich Skomorokhov recalled his impressions of the start of the battle:

> Everything was standing on end and had begun to make a thunderous noise – the Hitlerites had rushed into a counter-attack, inflicting their principal attack between Lakes Velentse and Balaton. After they had broken through our first defensive line with their powerful, armored fists, they set off for the Danube. The final defensive operation fought by Soviet forces began, which was known as the Balaton Operation. In order to rein in the enemy, the Front Line Commander put all his available forces into battle, even a division of the slow, Po-2 night bombers. We pilots found ourselves having to fight around the clock.

The following day, the Germans reinforced their attacking formations. Marshal Tolbukhin had not employed all his 3rd Ukrainian Front reserve but had strengthened his defenses. In the midest of this severe fighting, the Soviet leadership decided to organize a celebration in honor of International Women's Day, the first to be celebrated since the start of the war. Armorer E.V. Brovkina, of the 951st Ground Attack Air Regiment, which was deployed in the Hungarian village of Tekel, with women and girls making up a significant part of the technical personnel, recalled how this day was celebrated:

> Everyone of course was happy – they began to make some noise and talk loudly amongst themselves. They worried too of course because we did have dresses, but with slippers – nightmare! We had nothing [else] and that was it! We had to go to a ball in our slippers. On the morning of 8 March everyone was in a good mood. Finally, our work was done – the guns and machine guns had been cleaned, the ammunition loaded. We could relax; we had an evening's celebration ahead of us.
>
> Alas on that day Flight Commander Lieutenant German Odnotsenov failed to return from his sortie. Naturally, our joy was dispelled slightly. We met the girls from the 672nd Regiment – they were happy and joking amongst themselves, and among them was the wife of the deceased pilot. They had got married only very recently! We decided however not to tell her what had happened with the Germans. Odnotsenov was subsequently awarded the title of Hero of the Soviet Union posthumously.
>
> The girls took off their cotton trousers and greasy jackets, which had been smeared in oil and kerosene, and their enormous, insulated sleeves, and from soldiers they turned into beautiful girls. Their smiles began to radiate, their girlish faces began to redden and their eyes began to sparkle. We proposed toasts, congratulated the girls, and expressed our thanks for their work. Then the dancing began. The entire regiment was waltzing around the floor!

The intensity of Soviet sorties throughout 8 March was higher than on the two preceding days, due to the weather improving slightly and the identification of the enemy's main breakthrough. "Despite the heavy losses, in places on 8 March the enemy's tank spearheads drove further into our own battle lines by some 3 to 5 kilometers," recalled G.P. Yevdokimov, who was then a squadron navigator in the 449th Bomber Air Regiment. The most difficult situation was in the area around the settlement of Seregélyes and south of Nagybajom. Soviet aerial reconnaissance revealed that the Germans had concentrated a large amount of personnel and military hardware there. General Sudets, commander of the 17th Air Army, made the decision to immediately attack the opposing forces around Seregélyes using the 306th Ground Attack Air Division, and around Nagybajom with the 449th Bomber Regiment. Yevdokimov continued:

> The regimental commander [Major V.F. Tyushkevich] ordered us and Captain D.S. Yegorkin to head up the latter group of bombers. Thick smoke, low cloud and the rapidly changing situation on the front line made the execution of this combat mission considerably more difficult. Exceptional skill was required of all the pilots, as well as a high degree of accuracy so that they did not inflict friendly fire by mistake.
>
> Giving regimental commander his orders, divisional commander Colonel P.V. Nedosekin said: 'Warn the leading crew to be careful over the battlefield, our forces are fighting alongside' ... The cloud cover enabled them to reach an altitude of just 500m. The visibility was abysmal. The fact that the area was abundant in characteristic landmarks, such as the River Danube, and Lakes Balaton and Velentse, and the fact that this was not the first time we had flown here – all this meant that we knew many of the landmarks. I had no doubt that I would find the target. Something else was worrying me: the low altitude for this flight, at which not only could we be hit by anti-aircraft artillery, but actually any gunfire. I checked my calculations several times over to ensure the greatest degree of bombing accuracy. For half the transit to the target the cloud cover kept us below 400m – this was the minimum safe altitude for dropping our bombs.

At the target itself, when the crew of Yegorkin's Boston had already taken aim, the horizon began to be peppered with bunches of explosions – German anti-aircraft artillery were trying to throw the group off course. Then smoke trails from Oerlikon gun rockets began to snake towards the aircraft. Squadron navigator Yevdokimov reported to the pilot that the bombs had been dropped, after which he switched on the on-board camera. In places narrow strips of yellowish flame could be discerned through the blackout. As the aircraft turned away from the target, the bomber shook from a sudden blast and thick black smoke began to pour out of the starboard engine. The pilot flipped the aircraft onto its starboard wing and it began to continue flying close to the ground. Yegorkin managed, on one engine, to reach Tekel aerodrome, where he landed safely. According to post-mission photo interpretation data, 11 islands of fire were created in the area around the target and 14 vehicles were destroyed, as well as one tank and an armored personnel carrier. The German counter-attack had been stopped, for Sudets expressed his thanks to the entire complement of aircrew who had taken part in the sortie. A short time later, navigator Yevdokimov, who had flown 270 successful sorties (of which 76 were by day and the remainder night missions), was recommended for the title of Hero of the Soviet Union.

The 866th Fighter Air Regiment commander, Hero of the Soviet Union Captain A.I. Koldunov, was at this time named as one of the Red Army Air Force's best fighters. At the start of the German offensive near Lake Balaton, he was awarded the Order of the Patriotic War 1st Class. The recommendation stated that from 19 November 1944 to 14 February 1945, Koldunov had, "occasionally flying two or three mission sorties per day during the course of the battles on the approaches to Budapest, and crossing the Danube, and the encirclement of the Budapest alignment, and particularly in beating back the powerful enemy counter-attack", flown 60 mission sorties, personally shooting down 15 enemy aircraft.

The third day of the German offensive, 8 March, became one of the most successful days in the biography of this decorated Soviet ace. During the course of reconnaissance flights, he shot down three Bf 109s in two sorties, two of which wore Hungarian markings, while a third is thought to have belonged to the *I/JG53* group. After being taken prisoner, one of his victims, Senior Lieutenant Viktor Inken of *101/8 V.Szd*, was sure that he had been shot down by Soviet anti-aircraft artillery since the attack from his rear whad been so decisive and unexpected.

On the first day of the German offensive, the weather had not been conducive to aircraft operations. The cloud base then lifted and the intensity of aerial operations increased. Over the course of 7 and 8 March, the 17th Air Army of the 3rd Ukrainian Front flew 1,157 mission sorties, of which 229 were at night. Meanwhile, the 5th Air Army from the neighboring 2nd Ukrainian Front had flown 172 sorties to defend Soviet positions. The Soviet Air Force largely concentrated on the destruction of German tanks and personnel south of Lake Velentse. Over these three days, German and Hungarian pilots flew 183 sorties, in the course of which they carried out a number of large-scale attacks on Soviet defenses. The Red Army Air Force, whilst maintaining air superiority over the battlefield, had a profound effect on the course of the fighting by restricting the enemy in terms of the movement they could make in the hours of daylight. The Germans were also experiencing serious shortages of fuel, which prevented the *Luftwaffe* from using their forces to their fullest extent.

The Soviet Supreme High Command followed the course of Operation *Spring Awakening* with some concern. Chief of Staff General S.P. Ivanov recalled:

> On one occasion we and Lieutenant Colonel A.S. Zheltov, a Member of the Military Council for our front, were in the front line commander's office. At that time Marshal of the Soviet Union F.I. Tolbukhin had telephoned I.V. Stalin. He was interested in the situation, and particularly the composition and the alignment of enemy forces that had amassed against us. When [Tolbukhin] reported the information we had to hand that day, the Commander in Chief suddenly asked: 'Maybe pull the forces of the 3rd Ukrainian Front back to the eastern bank of the Danube?' The question was unexpected, and Tolbukhin asked for permission to answer him after half an hour. As a result of this exchange of ideas we came to the conclusion that pulling

> the forces back to the eastern bank of the Danube could lead to unexpected consequences. In the situation that had unfolded it would be more beneficial to stubbornly defend the positions that the troops had occupied at the stronghold. When Tolbukhin reported this to Stalin he agreed with our conclusions and approved the decision the front-line commander had made over the defense.

When Marshal Tolbukhin asked Headquarters to allow him, when necessary, to introduce the 9th Guards Army, that had just been transferred from the 2nd Ukrainian Front, into the battle, his request was categorically denied. In a directive dated 9 March 1945, in which the preceding order had been repeated – to wipe out the enemy's tank alignment in defensive battles no later than 15–16 March and then to go on the offensive using the right wing of the front line – Stalin and Chief of the General Staff General A.I. Antonov indicated: "The 9th Guards Army should not be drawn into the defensive battles but should be used to build on the success and for the final routing of the enemy."

Despite heavy losses, German ground forces still tried to break through to the Danube on 10 March, and on the subsequent five days. Judging by the fragmented reports written by the *Luftwaffe*'s Quartermaster-General, the Germans had also incurred considerable losses in the air as well – just the previous day, the *SG 10* squadron had lost six FW 190s. The intensity of the battles had, it seemed, reached its zenith. The thunder of artillery fire, clatter of tanks tracks and roar of the engines from ground-attack aircraft did not let up even for a minute. The pilots never got out of their cockpits between sorties, taking off again and again to support and cover ground forces. In one day, the crews of the 17th Air Army flew between 800 and 900 mission sorties. As before, the ground-attack aircraft operated with a high degree of intensity. Thus, on 13 March, a group of Ils from the 672nd Ground Attack Air Regiment (306th Ground Attack Air Division) carried out a bombing raid on a concentration of German tanks and personnel in the Bokon–Kolon area. The target was fiercely protected by anti-aircraft artillery, but, despite this, the Soviet pilots were able to maneuver around the ground fire and continued with the attack. Lieutenant G.G. Cherkashin distinguished himself that day, destroying one tank and two armored personnel carriers loaded with troops.

Grigory Grigoryevich Cherkashin, who was awarded the title of Hero of the Soviet Union after the war, recalled:

> The battles near Balaton were severe; it was there that the Sixth Panzer Army abandoned their tanks. At the end of April, when the battle here had already come to a close, an unusual, and even amusing investigation was held, into who had destroyed a column of German heavy tanks. Our regiment had bombed and blanketed this target twice. Some of the tanks had caught fire, while the others had stopped, immobilized, [and] the Germans abandoned them and fled, wherever they could go. Owing to these 'Tigers' a full-on argument broke out between us and the tank crews. They wrote reports to the effect that they had fired on the Germans from an ambush. Our Commander in Chief General V.A. Sudets became involved, sending a commission, which recorded: the holes in the armor were from aerial anti-tank bombs and rockets, so it was the ground-attack aircraft that had finished them off.

Cherkashin went on to admit that on more than one occasion, he had been confronted with a dangerous situation in March 1945:

> I thought that the enemy fighters would force me into Lake Balaton. There were a large number of fighters in the air at any one time but they did not engage us in open combat, but waited for the right moment, moving in and out of the clouds, isolating the outer aircraft in the formation, which they shot down. This was how they isolated me from the rest of the group as I was on my way back, so I let them chase me over the lake. I went down to low level and banked, but they dived down from overhead, so that they did not pass through the gunner's line of fire. My sixth sense saved me – at the last moment I banked away steeply, [and] the squirt of fire passed to the right of me. Then the Messerschmitt's wingman attacked me from the port side. I then banked away again, but this time to the other side.
>
> I could not keep this up for long; I was gradually losing speed, it was already almost at landing speed, and I could count the propeller blades as they rotated and see the shadow of the enemy fighter on the water. I understood that he was after me, and I began to increase speed gradually – I could not do this quickly, since the aircraft would enter a spin. When the speed was sufficient for an energetic maneuver, I turned my aircraft back onto the German, who ended up alongside me. I looked – he was in my sight, I pressed the trigger switch and the enemy fighter exploded. His wingman had already got away ... I experienced many dangerous episodes like these in my life on the front line [in total over the course of the war he flew 240 sorties], and sometimes they were scary, but my most dangerous tests were over Lake Balaton.

The different branches of the Red Army cooperated superbly to help the Soviet troops to survive their predicament. For example, thanks to systematic and careful reconnaissance (both aerial and ground), the artillery succeeded in planning and executing a maneuver which had a decisive effect on the success of the 57th Army's defense; moving the batteries up to the threatened sectors continued for the first four or five days of the operation. The density of artillery fire south of Nagybajom – in the southern defensive sector – grew rapidly. If by the start of the battle there were eight guns and mortars per kilometer of the front, then by the morning of 7 March this had risen to 47, on the third day it reached 87 and on the fifth day there were some 112 every kilometer along the line of combat. In total in this sector there were up to 690 guns and mortars of various calibers; consequently, it would have been impossible for the Germans to colntinue their advance without incurring enormous losses.

After halting the enemy's onslaught, the Soviet Air Force continued to increase the strength of their attacks, as recorded by the combat diary of the German 5th SS Panzer Division *Wiking*:

> On 16 March 1945, all hell broke loose. By the middle of the day the Soviets were raining mortar fire down onto German artillery positions. On the village of Csor south-west of Székesfehérvár there were two light batteries with six 10.5cm field howitzers ... The batteries were subjected to such a powerful bombardment, which the rank and file artillerymen had never seen before. It was true that the raid only lasted for one hour, but it seemed to go on forever. The houses around the artillery positions were destroyed. The shrapnel from the shells flew in different directions, and there was barely time to evacuate the wounded. The telephony cables were severed after the first few direct hits, and all communications were lost. It was impossible to communicate with the front line, or the [commander] *Standartenfuhrer* T. Bünning, or with artillery regiment headquarters, or even with our own detachments.

After 'teething troubles' had been eradicated for the new aircraft that had been brought into service with the 17th Air Army, the enhancement in the strength of the Yak-3 aircraft – the most widespread new aircraft type in Hungary – meant that this fighter occupied a prime position in the aerial formations and the best-trained pilots made use of its unusual qualities in air combat. The main advantage the Yak-3 held was its high maximum speed at low and medium altitudes, while it also had excellent vertical maneuverability. As a rule, pilots flying this aircraft would engage the enemy in combat using ascending maneuvers. Documents state that Hero of the Soviet Union Major A.I. Koldunov from the 866th Fighter Air Regiment set an example for his comrades when he shot down three Bf 109s on 17 March.

Considering the high level of training of the pilots in his group, Major Koldunov employed high-speed maneuvers, attacking the enemy in the pursuit, chasing them in the vertical climb and using combat turns. Koldunov considered an attack from above the most complicated approach, since the aircraft drew fatally close to one another, and as it was necessary to fire from short range, there was a real danger of a collision with the enemy aircraft on the exit from the attack. Therefore, this required careful and assiduous pilot training, as well as monitoring the execution of combat training maneuvers.

As had occurred before, it was predominantly the young, insufficiently trained Soviet crews who perished during these operations. On 18 March, however, the squadron commander of the 165th Guards Ground Attack Air Regiment (10th Guards Ground Attack Air Division), Captain I.D. Pavlov, was killed when his 'Il' exploded in mid-air over the target after a direct hit from an anti-aircraft shell. This was the pilot's 133rd sortie since he had made his debut in December 1942, and he was posthumously awarded the title of Hero of the Soviet Union. The following day, the deputy commander of the 866th Fighter Air Regiment (288th Fighter Air Division), Major I.F. Chyorniy, was also killed by ground fire near the village of Csor. On 21 March, *Luftwaffe* fighter aircraft, taking advantage of a mistake by escorting Soviet fighters, hit an Il-2 from close range which was piloted by the commander of the 210th Ground Attack Air Regiment (136th Ground Attack Air Division), Major A.L. Kondratkov.

The table below provides figures on the number of mission sorties and enemy incursions on the most active days for the

Date	17th Air Army sorties	17th Air army victories	5th Air Army sorties	Including those flown in the interests of the 3rd Ukrainian Front	5th Air Army victories	Total number shot down	Enemy incursions	Notes
8 March	887	19	?	76	?	19	107	Enemy aviation attacked in groups of between 20 and 25 aircraft.
9 March	874	10	280	260	9	28	187	
11 March	990	21	407	298	–	25	103	Four aircraft were shot down by infantry fire from the guns of the 3rd Ukrainian Front
13 March	796	12	222	190	?	14	more than 100	
14 March	727	11	?	66	1	15	up to 100	
16 March	536	19	–	–	–	20	200	
18 March	1,148	23	625	?	4	40	130	The *Luftwaffe*, according to their own data, flew 400 mission sorties that day
19 March	1,091	22	583	?	7	32	78	
20 March	1,120	14	868	?	17	31	145	

Soviet air forces near Balaton, based on operational reports from Red Army General Headquarters:

The interim results of the fight for Balaton were summed up by Stalin. In an order dated 24 March 1945, he noted that the troops of the 3rd Ukrainian Front, having beaten back attacks by 11 German *panzer* divisions south-west of Budapest and worn them down in defensive battles, then went on the offensive, routing a German *panzer* group and advancing 70km on a more than 100km-long front; they had then occupied the large cities of Székesfehérvár and Veszprom, and more than 350 other settlements, taking more than 6,000 enemy officers and men prisoner. The Soviet formations destroyed, or captured 745 *panzers* and assault guns, more than 800 guns and many other weapons and pieces of military hardware. Having acknowledged the role of aviation in these victories, Stalin expressed his thanks to Sudets and N.M. Korsakov (the commander and Chief of Staff), andGenerals A.E. Zlatotsvetov, A.N. Vitruk, O.V. Tolstikov, S.I. Tishchenko, G.I. Belitsky and others who led the aviation corps and divisions in the 17th Air Army.

According to German sources, the *Luftwaffe*, despite their difficulties, did achieve a series of tactical successes, shooting down dozens of Soviet aircraft, including the latest types. The *Luftwaffe*'s best fighter group by far in this was *II/JG52*, which had been led since February 1942 by *kapitän* W. Batz. This group, unlike others, retained its outstanding aces, who by the onset of spring had achieved between 56 and 227 victories. Over the course of March 1945, they shot down 41 more Soviet aircraft, and furthermore a 'series' is occasionally noted in the documents when they were 'free hunting'. Thus, *Leutnant* P. Duettmann shot down six aircraft of various types on 11 March, then on 16 March he claimed five more Il-2s. German losses at this time, however, were considerable: up to 22 Messerschmitts had to be written off in the space of a month, with seven pilots killed or missing without trace, while five men, including Duettmann and another ace, *Leutnant* H. Ewald, were injured.

Hungarian fighter pilots also increased their personal tallies considerably during this period. A comparison of the descriptions of the same battles in Hungarian and Soviet sources gives rise to curious results. For example, the Hungarians assert that on 9 March, a group of eight Bf 109Gs from *101/8 V.Szd* attacked 25 Bostons near Polgárdi, which were being escorted by 16 Yak-9s, shooting down three of them. Soviet information confirms the fact of the attack, and the time and location, as well as the number of Messerschmitts that took part in the battle. It does not, however, confirm the loss of any of the bombers from the 260th Bomber Air Regiment; three aircraft were damaged, and one of the gunners was injured, but the only loss was Lieutenant Roya's aircraft, the engine of which caught fire on take-off, forcing the pilot to landed near Sombor aerodrome, after which the aircraft burnt out. Neither do Soviet documents confirm the loss of any of the escort fighters from the 288th Fighter Air Division. On the other hand, Soviet sources consistently attest that return fire brought down two of the Bf 109s that had attacked the formation, which the Hungarians did not acknowledge. Furthermore, Soviet crews noted seven explosions caused by the raid, plus up to 19 islands of fire, near the settlement of Polgárdi.

Throughout the March fighting, not only the Red Army Air Force and the Anglo–American air forces, but also the Hungarians did not reduce their activity, although interruptions in the supply of fuel had an effect on the intensity of the latter's combat activity. Their sorties were predominantly flown to engage in 'free hunting', and their most successful day was 22 March, when the Hungarians claimed that they had downed 27 Soviet aircraft. However, only a day later, as they were flying from Vezsprom to Szombathely, landing on a runway that had been damaged as a result of bombing and strafing raids led to disaster for the Hungarians: 26 Messerschmitts were damaged, and since there was no way they could be repaired or evacuated, they all had to be blown up. On 13 March, *Ober-Leutnant* F. Malnashi was killed in action (having attained 15 victories), and five days later *Feldwebel* L. Budai (who had nine victories to his name) and another ace, *Unter-Offizier* D. Schikora, sustained serious injuries and could not participate in subsequent air battles.

This chronicle has concentrated on the actions of German and Hungarian fighters and ground-attack aircraft. Nevertheless, other types of aviation also played an important role for both countries. Documents captured from the *NSGr5* groups of night bombers reveal that quite a number of experienced, well-trained crews remained in the group who were still capable of flying sorties in bad weather conditions. During the course of the battles near Lake Balaton, the group, led by *Major* J. Boellner, had approximately 50 Ar 66s and Go 145s, and flew from aerodromes at Komarno, Várpalota and Balbanapusti. In the first three months of 1945, they lost 13 of these aircraft, of which 10 were left for various reasons in the area around Budapest, since they had not been able to get out of the pocket, while three other crews disappeared without trace. Fuel limitations led to it being quite rare for more than one sortie a day to be flown, even though they had the capability to fly two or even three sorties daily.

Although the war was coming to a victorious end for the Soviets, the operational situation in Hungary remained probably the most strained it had been, despite the fact that the *Luftwafffe*'s principal forces were by then located in Germany as part of the 6th Air Fleet. According to a report by the headquarters of the Red Army Air Force, in March 1945 formations under Colonel General Sudets incurred the highest losses as they underwent conversion to combat mission sorties, compared to other air armies:

The 17th Air Army, supporting the forces of the 3rd Ukrainian Front in the defensive battles in the area around Székesfehérvár and the subsequent offensive against Győr, Szombathely and Vienna, flew 20,471 mission sorties, or approximately four times more than the previous month, and lost 169 aircraft [a further 137 combat aircraft had to be written off as a result of accidents]. Thus, they flew 121 mission sorties for each aircraft lost, against 173 mission sorties in February. Casualties among bomber and ground-attack aviation aircraft and crews increased considerably, for the most part due to anti-aircraft artillery fire.

Oberst-Gruppenführer SS and Colonel-General of SS troops Josef Dietrich commanded the Sixth Panzer Army during the course of the Spring Awakening battles. Under his leadership, troops using Tiger-II, Panzerjäger Tiger and Panther tanks in intensive attacks,succeeded in breaking through two echelons of the Soviet defense, but were not able to fulfil the task they had been set to reach the Danube, for which Dietrich incurred the wrath of Hitler.

Self-propelled *Wirbelwind* anti-aircraft guns augmented the German armored columns' anti-aircraft defenses during the battle for Balaton. They are seen here at Székesfehérvár in March 1945.

A Pe-2 Soviet reconnaissance aircraft in the skies above Hungary follows the progress of enemy columns.

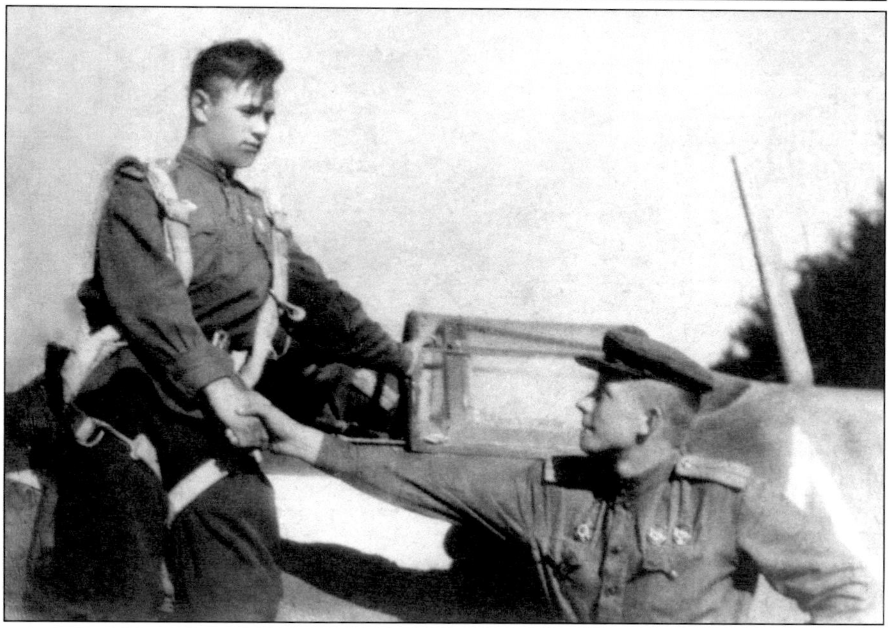

V.V. Kirilyuk congratulates his regimental colleague in the 31st Fighter Air Regiment, N.M. Skomorokhov, on the successful completion of his sortie.

Senior Lieutenant I.L. Mogilchak from the 235th Ground Attack Air Regiment, V Ground Attack Air Corps, was awarded the Gold Star in February 1944. The then Major Ivan Mogilchak's aircraft was shot down over Budapest on his 140th sortie, and he was forced to make an emergency landing. He died in hospital on 14 February 1945 from wounds and burns he sustained in the incident.

An example of the German armored military hardware destroyed near Lake Velentse in March 1945.

The newest BF 109G-14s, manufactured in Hungary under license from Germany, were ready for battle during the operation.

With the aircraft having taken to the skies and the aerodrome being left empty, a Hungarian technician rests on boxes of technical equipment waiting for the group to return.

Pilots of the 31st Guards Fighter Air Regiment, 6th Guards Fighter Air Division, standing next to a new Yak-9U fighter. In the center is Senior Lieutenant N.I. Nikulin.

This ZSU-37 Möbelwagen self-propelled gun belonged to the 509th Panzer Battalion and was destroyed as a result of an attack by Soviet ground-attack aircraft.

Soviet anti-aircraft crews protected the bridges across the Danube in Budapest.

These two photographs and the two opposite are examples of Hungarian aircraft technology captured in the course of the Red Army's offensive. The Hungarians blew up many of these as they withdrew, while others became unserviceable as a result of accidents and were abandoned. Even aircraft such as the most modern versions of the Bf 109G were captured.

Damaged or unserviceable tanks were brought to Székesfehérvár, as were assault guns and armored personnel carriers that were abandoned after the defeat of the German and Hungarian forces in the battle for Lake Balaton.

Destroyed German and Hungarian aircraft at the end of the war.

Personnel from the 897th Fighter Air Regiment (228th Fighter Air Division) at the end of the war. In the front row, sixth from the right, is the regiment's most successful ace, twice Hero of the Soviet Union Captain A.I. Koldunov.

Balatonalmádi station, on the shores of Lake Balaton, south-east of Veszprém, was a large supply base for the German forces ahead of the counter-attack. The view of the station after the defeat of the German Sixth Panzer Army and the withdrawal of German forces also shows the results of Soviet Air Force raids.

Pilots of the Soviet 164th Fighter Air Regiment (10thGround Attack Air Corps) rest in the spring sunshine next to a new La-7 fighter. In the background is a Po-2 communication aircraft.

This Yak-3 was manufactured outside of planned fighter production and was donated by the workers of factory No. 292 in Saratov to the commander of the 2nd Ukrainian Front, Marshal R.Y. Malinovsky. He in turn handed it over ceremoniously to a young pilot, Junior Lieutenant V.G. Lapshin of the 150th Guards Fighter Air Regiment (III Guards Fighter Air Corps), who shot down two enemy aircraft over Budapest, for which he was awarded the Order of the Red Banner.

A Hungarian pilot poses next to a Bf-109G-14AS fighter shortly before the end of the war.

Conclusion

The forces of the 2nd Ukrainian Front entered Hungarian sovereign territory on 23 September 1944. From that date until 4 April 1945, when the territory of the nation was successfully purged of Nazis, Soviet forces carried out three offensives (the Debrecen, Budapest, and Vienna operations), as well as one defensive operation (the Balaton operation). During the course of these, the troops of the 2nd and 3rd Ukrainian Fronts routed large enemy formations. The battles in Hungary involving tanks and motorized formations, as well as large numbers of aircraft, were characterized by their excessive severity and bloodshed.

As a result of these actions, the Germans lost their last remaining ally, and the pre-requisites were created for concluding attacks against Hitler's forces in Austria and Czechoslovakia. Yet victory was handed to the Red Army at a high price: the irrevocable losses alone for Soviet armed forces on Hungarian territory were almost 140,000 officers and men. Much has already been said about the possible scale of aircraft losses. Soviet documents assert that from October 1944 to March 1945, units and detachments of the 5th and 17th Air armies lost more than 1,250 combat aircraft for various reasons; hundreds of crews were either killed or lost without trace.

Undoubtedly, the *Luftwaffe* also paid a high price in this battle, but no accurate figures are available concerning their losses. While Hungarian ground forces from the end of 1944 until the beginning of 1945 refused to engage with Soviet forces and even defected to their side, the core of the Royal Hungarian Air Force remained loyally on the German side until the end of the war – around 80 Hungarian fighter and ground-attack aircraft crews continued to fight the Red Army Air Force after having abandoned the aerodromes in their own country, flying from bases in Austria and Czechoslovakia. The final claim for a victory made by a Hungarian pilot (the aircraft that was shot down was identified as a Yak-9) was submitted on 17 April 1945, when the war in Europe had just days to go.

But despite the considerable skill of German aces piloting different types of aircraft – from fighters to ground-attack aircraft – and the stubborn nature of the Hungarian aviators, in the end they could not have any bearing on the outcome of the air battle across the entire front.

The central district of Budapest after the surrender of the encircled garrison. The Hungarian tricolor is shown flying over the city.

The western edge of the Hungarian capital, in a view taken from a Po-2 aircraft.

Twice Hero of the Soviet Union V.N. Osipov from fought in an Il-4 from June 1941 as part of the 81st (subsequently the 5th Guards) Bomber Air Regiment, 18th Air Army (up until December 1944 this was part of the Soviets' long-range aviation forces). He flew 412 sorties, including 382 at night, and 16 against long-range targets; he even bombed Budapest. He ended the war as part of the 26th Guards Bomber Air Regiment, flying Li-2 and Mitchell bombers.

Twice Hero of the Soviet Union Captain K.A. Yevstigneyev of the 178th Guards Fighter Air Regiment (14th Guards Fighter Air Division) attained five personal victories and set an enemy aerostat on fire in the battles over Budapest and western Hungary. By the end of the war, Kirill Alekseyevich Yevstigneyev had become one of the most tactically adept Soviet aces, constantly demonstrating his flying skill, and resourcefulness.

The German ace Major Erich Hartmann climbs out of the cockpit of his Messerschmitt after attaining his 337th victory. By the end of the war in May 1945, he had 352 aerial victories to his name.

The Hungarian ace Kalman Istvan brought his tally of 'kills' up to 12 during Operation Spring Awakening.

Once the bloody battles had come to an end, the population of Budapest committed the bodies of many of the fallen to the earth.

A commemorative plaque at the school in Vyaznikov in honor of its alumnus, the Soviet ace N.F. Krasnov and the tank commander I.P. Korchagin, who were both born there.

Senior Lieutenant I.I. Grigoryev from the 93rd Guards Ground Attack Air Regiment (II Guards Ground Attack Air Corps), who first fought in April 1943, distinguished himself in the winter of 1944/45 over Hungary, successfully leading detachments of between six and eight Il-2s. Ivan Ivanovich Grigoryev was shot down by ground fire near the Polish town of Częstochowa on 8 May 1945, the last day of the war. He bailed out of his aircraft but had insufficient altitude for the parachute canopy to inflate and was killed. He was buried with full military honors and was posthumously awarded the title of Hero of the Soviet Union.

Lieutenant N.I. Dynich of the 513th Fighter Air Regiment, 331st Fighter Air Division, stands on the wing of a Yak-9 fighter after a sortie. During the battles in Hungary, the regiment's fighter pilots were almost exclusively concentrating on escorting the aircraft of the V Ground Attack Air Corps.

Two pilots from the 897th Fighter Air Regiment clarify their forthcoming sortie on a map board. In the foreground is a Yak-3 aircraft, with which the regiment was fully equipped at the end of the war.

5-13. Lieutenant N. Kochetov's Yak-9D fighter aircraft from the 31st Guards Fighter Air Regiment.

Captain A.M. Kuchumov of the 451st Ground Attack Air Regiment, who flew 215 mission sorties in an Il-2 aircraft, attacking Axis personnel and hardware from low level. After the capture of Budapest, Kuchumov was recommended for the title of Hero of the Soviet Union. He is shown retrieving his parachute from the cockpit after a sortie.

Romanian pilots from the I Air Corps who received Soviet awards in March 1945 congratulate one another and look forward to a rapid conclusion to the war.

This Yak-3 fighter manufactured as a result of private donations, with the inscription 'From Ferapont Petrovich Golovatov, the 2nd aircraft for the final defeat of the enemy!', ended up in a museum. The deputy commander of the 6th Guards Fighter Air Division, Lieutenant Colonel B.N. Yeremin, flew this aircraft until the end of the war. Subsequently, the aircraft was exhibited in the A.S. Yakovlev OKB museum on the Leningrad Prospekt in Moscow, but currently sits in the Vadim Zadorozhniy Technical Museum at Krasnogorsk near Moscow.

A Soviet major, awarded a medal for his part in the capture of Budapest, photographed in the city on Attila Street. The city's inhabitants can be seen returning to their peaceful lives, together with a glider that has crashed into a house after an unsuccessful landing.

A pit of smashed German and Hungarian hardware at Balaton station. It is evident that many of the tanks and armored personnel carriers have fallen victim to direct hits by 2.5kg cumulative bombs.

Junior Sergeant P.F. Gladishka, an armorer in the 31st Fighter Air Regiment (295th Fighter Air Division), criss-crossed with ammunition belts, stands next to an La-5 aircraft bearing the inscription 'The Novomoskovsk Collective Farm Worker'.

A section of the 92nd Guards Ground Attack Air Regiment (4th Guards Air Division, 5th Air Army). On the right is the regimental Chief of Staff.

A transport aviation aerodrome, from where fuel was delivered on Junkers-52 aircraft to the encircled garrison. Hungarian soldiers and officers can be seen on the aerodrome.

Fighter pilot I.S. Prozor of the 85th Guard's Fighter Air Regiment stands next to his Yak-1. Spring 1945.

A group of 73rd Guards Fighter Air Regiment (III Guards Fighter Air Corps) pilots standing next to a Yak-9 aircraft bearing the inscription 'From the workers of Kiev'. In the cockpit is Lieutenant I.V. Starikov.

A building and a devastated courtyard on Yunash-Andor Street after the conclusion of the battle for Budapest in March 1945.

The famous Soviet photojournalist E.A. Khaldey was impressed by the departure of Il-2 ground-attack aircraft on a mission sortie on the 3rd Ukrainian Front.

Senior Lieutenant A.N. Adgantsev of the 150th Guards Fighter Air Regiment descends from the cockpit of a Yak-3 following a sortie. By the end of February 1945, the pilot has recorded nine personal and four joint victories in his tally and flown approximately 100 sorties.

Appendix I

Luftwaffe Fleet 4 Combat Strength

Formation	Commander	Regiments	Aircraft types
St./FAGr4	*Maj.* H.-D. Klette	*3(F)/121, 3(F)/33, 1(F)/Nacht*	Ju 188, Do 217, He 111
St./KG4	*Obstlt* W. Klosinski	*II, III/KG4*	He 111
I Air Corps	*Gen.* P. Deichmann		
St./NAGr4	*Maj.* H. Barsikow		Bf 109
St./SG2	*Obstlt* H.-U. Rudel	*I, II, III, 10(Pz.)/SG2*	FW 190, Ju 87
St./SG10	*Obstlt* E. Janssen	*I, II, III/SG10*	FW 190
St./NSGr5	*Maj.* J. Böllner		Ar 66, Go 145, Ju 87
St./JG76	*Maj.* E. Düllberg	*II/JG51, II/JG52, I/JG53*	Bf 109
		10(Pz.), 14(Pz.)/SG9	Hs 129
		2/NAGr16	FW 189

Appendix II

Soviet 5th Air Army Combat Strength

Formations	Commander	Regiments	Aircraft types
V ShaK	Major General N.P. Kamanin		
4th Guards ShAD	Colonel V.F. Saprykin	90th, 91st, 92nd Guards ShAP	Il-2
264th ShAD	Colonel E.V. Klobukov	235th, 451st, 809th ShAP	Il-2
331st IAD	Colonel I.A. Semenenko	122nd, 179th, 513th IAP	Yak-9
III Guards ShAK	Lieutenant General V.V. Stepichev		
7th Guards ShAD	Colonel G.P. Shuteev	130th, 131st, 132nd Guards ShAP	Il-2
12th Guards ShAD	Colonel L.A. Chizhikov	187th, 188th, 190th Guards ShAP	Il-2
279th IAD	Colonel V.G. Blagoveshchensky	92nd, 192nd, 486th IAP	La-5
III Guards IAK	Lieutenant General I.D. Podgorny		
13th Guards IAD	Colonel I.A. Taranenko	177th, 178th, 179th Guards IAP	La-5, La-7
14th Guards IAD	Colonel A.P. Yudakov	149th, 150th, 151st Guards IAP	Yak-9
6th Guards IAD	Colonel I.I. Geibo	31st, 73rd, 85th Guards IAP	Yak-9, Yak-3
218th BAD	Colonel N.K. Romanov	48th, 452nd, 453rd BAP	A-20B, A-20G
312th NBAD	Colonel V.P. Chanpalov	392nd, 930th, 992nd Air Regiments	Po-2
		511th ORAP	Pe-2
		207th OKRAP	Il-2, Yak-9
		95th TrAP	Po-2
		18th GVF Air Regiment	Po-2
		85th, 1001st Medical Air Regiment	Po-2

ShAK Attack Air Corps
ShAD Attack Air Division
ShAP Attack Air Regiment
IAK Fighter Air Corps
IAD Fighter Air Division
IAP Fighter Air Regiment
BAD Bomber Air Division
NBAD Night Bomber Air Division
BAP Bomber Air Regiment
ORAP Separate Reconnaissance Air Regiment
TrAP Transportation Air Regiment
GVF Civil Air Fleet
OKRAP Separate Observation and Reconnaissance Air Regiment